Woman in the Wake

A Novel By Ciera Dupuis

About the Author

Ciera is a writer, mother, and voice for women rediscovering their power. With a heart rooted in faith and a life shaped by seasons of both challenge and growth, she believes in the beauty of beginning again—not just once, but as many times as it takes.

Her writing speaks to the quiet strength that lives in every woman—the strength to pause, reflect, rise, and rebuild. Through her storytelling, Ciera encourages readers to look inward with compassion, to honor every chapter of their lives, and to understand that healing doesn't mean forgetting—it means evolving.

This is not a story of heartbreak; it's a story of becoming.

A reminder that life is not about erasing the past but embracing the truth that we are all unfolding. Daily. Boldly. Gently.

With two young sons as her guiding light, she writes for the women who carry the world on their shoulders and still dare to dream. Her passion lies in empowering others to own their voices, trust their timing, and rise in their own way—even if it starts with a whisper.

She is living proof that your story isn't over—and it never was.

Dedication

To my sons —

You are the reason I kept going when I thought I couldn't.

You are the light that guided me through the darkest chapters.

The joy that reminded me of who I am,

And the hope that carried me into the woman I was always meant to be.

This story is my gift to you —

A testament to the strength we carry in our hearts,

The risks we take for love,

And the power of starting over.

May you always know that you were never a burden,

But always my purpose.

You are my everything.

With all my love,
Mom.

Table of Contents

Introduction: This Is Not a Story of Loss 1

Chapter 1: The Breaking 4

Chapter 2: Unraveled 19

Chapter 3: A Good Enough Goodbye 32

Chapter 4: Where the Quiet Lives 43

Chapter 5: All the Things I Didn't Say 54

Chapter 6: Salt in the Wound 67

Chapter 7: The Blur 80

Chapter 8: The Mom Group 90

Chapter 9: Running From Home 108

Chapter 10: Hollow Girl Era 144

Chapter 11: Making Room 153

Chapter 12: Let That Girl Burn 159

Chapter 13: A Different Kind of Love Story 166

Conclusion: The Wake 173

Introduction:
This Is Not a Story of Loss

Life rarely unfolds the way we plan. It stretches us, breaks us, and then asks us to rise—again and again. But we are not here to simply survive the breaking. We are here to become something more because of it.

This story is about a woman named Layla. But it could be about any woman who has ever stood at a crossroads—grieving the life she thought she'd have while reaching, however shakily, for something more. This is a story of rediscovery, of learning to trust yourself when the map is gone, and of understanding that sometimes, love continues in silence—and that's okay. Because not all closure comes in words, and not all strength roars. Sometimes, it simply begins with a quiet, courageous step forward.

Layla's journey is not about perfection or fairy-tale endings. It's about the sacred, messy, ongoing work of growth. It's a reminder that healing is not a destination but a path that unfolds daily. That you don't have to erase your past to honor your future. That the woman you are becoming is already within you, waiting for your permission.

This is not a story of loss. It is a story of becoming.

Though fictionalized, Layla's experience is woven from real threads—my own and those of countless women who have whispered truths into the dark and decided to begin again anyway. It's for the ones who've fallen, gotten back up, and are still learning to stand taller.

For the women who are mothers, who are daughters, who are partners, or walking alone.
For the ones who are healing, searching, building, remembering, or just beginning.
You are not alone. You are not too late. And you are not broken.

You are unfolding.

And this—this is only the beginning.

Chapter 1:
The Breaking

Layla stared at the plane ticket, her eyes fixating on the one-way label printed in bold, glaring against the otherwise ordinary countertop. It felt almost too surreal, too final. A single piece of paper, but one that carried the weight of her entire future on it. She reached out with trembling fingers and ran her thumb along the edges, feeling the smooth, crisp surface of the ticket. It was pristine—unmarked, untouched, brand new. Unlike her. Unlike the life she had lived.

She stood in the quiet kitchen, the hum of the refrigerator the only sound filling the stillness around her. Outside, the world was bustling with the sounds of life, but here, in this room, it felt as though time had stopped. Layla's gaze wandered over the ticket once more, but her thoughts quickly returned to the reality that had driven her here. In her arms, her youngest son, Noah, stirred restlessly. His small, chubby hands grabbed at her sleeve, his face scrunching up in discontent, sensing the shift in energy. Layla adjusted her hold on him as he squirmed, the familiar feeling of his warmth against her chest momentarily grounding her. At her side, Mia clung to her with the quiet desperation of a child who could sense something was amiss. Her small hand tugged at Layla's shirt, pulling her closer, her innocent face filled with confusion, asking questions her mother couldn't yet answer.

The ticket was for tomorrow's flight—a one-way escape from everything that had broken her. It was a literal and figurative departure, the weight of the decision pressing on her chest like a lead balloon. The excitement that had originally fluttered in her chest felt distant now, replaced by a quiet sense of uncertainty. But this escape wasn't just about the island she was heading to, this small, faraway place that promised a new beginning. It was about the life she had promised herself. A life free from the heartbreak she had endured, from the betrayal that had eroded her trust, and from the constant reminder that the life she had dreamed of—the perfect family—had slipped through her fingers like sand.

Layla closed her eyes and took a slow breath, the air thick and heavy in her lungs. She could feel her heart beating faster, the weight of the decision she had made settling heavily in her chest. She wasn't sure what the next chapter of her life would hold, but it had to be better than what she was leaving behind. It had to be. She couldn't keep living this life of quiet despair, of pretending that everything was okay when it wasn't. The broken pieces of her past had to be left behind, and she had to move forward, no matter how terrifying the future felt.

Her mother had called three times already that morning, each time a reminder of the ties she was cutting, the roots she was severing. Layla had let the phone ring out each time, the sound of her mother's concern echoing in the silence. What could she possibly say? That she was really going through with it? That she was leaving? That the girl who had followed love into heartbreak was finally, desperately, following herself out of it? The girl who had worked so hard to build a perfect family—only to watch it crumble—was now leaving the wreckage behind.

She couldn't bring herself to tell her mother yet. Not when everything still felt so raw, not when the decision was still so fresh. How could she explain that it wasn't just about the island? It was about her. It was about Mia and Noah. It was about finding herself again and, in doing so, giving them the life they deserved.

Layla slowly moved to the counter and placed the plane ticket carefully next to her purse. She lingered there for a moment, her eyes tracing the edges of the paper again as if somehow it could offer her the answers she sought. But it didn't. Instead, it only served as a painful reminder of everything she was walking away from—and everything she was walking toward. The house was nearly packed, the majority of their belongings already stuffed into a few hastily thrown-together bags. She had spent the last few days working through it all, organizing what she could salvage and deciding what to leave behind.

Yet, even now, as she stood in the kitchen, the reality of the move hadn't quite sunk in. She had taken the step, but the magnitude of it was still too heavy to comprehend.

Just as she was lost in her thoughts, the quiet hum of her phone snapped her back to the present. The screen lit up, and she saw her mother's name flashing again. Another call. Layla sighed, long and deep, her shoulders slumping slightly under the weight of it all. She had been avoiding it all morning, but she couldn't keep running forever. With a long, reluctant breath, Layla picked up the phone. She hesitated for just a moment before pressing "accept," the familiar sound of her mother's voice instantly filling the silence on the other end. It was enough to make Layla's stomach knot, her heart racing with the mix of guilt and dread that always seemed to follow these conversations.

"Layla, honey, I've called you three times this morning," her mother said, her voice thick with concern and confusion. "What's going on? You haven't said anything about this trip. Is everything okay?"

Layla stood there for a long moment, her breath catching in her chest. She wanted to tell her everything—the reasons, the emotions, the battles she had fought just to get to this point. She wanted to tell her mother how badly she needed this. How exhausted she was. How broken she had felt for so long. But the words wouldn't come. They caught in her throat like they always did when she tried to explain what she was feeling. Instead, she took a shaky breath and said the only thing she could manage, "I'm fine, Mom. I just—" She paused, her eyes drifting to the half-packed suitcase sitting on the floor, the reality of her situation sinking in just a little deeper. "I just need some space. Some time away."

"Time away?" Her mother's voice sharpened, the concern deepening with each word. "From what? You know you can talk to me about anything. I've been worried ever since you called to tell me you were thinking about this."

Layla swallowed hard. Her heart raced again, but this time, she held her ground. She wasn't ready to say everything, but she knew she couldn't keep hiding from the truth, either. "I'm going to start fresh, Mom. I'm doing this for me. For Mia and Noah." Her words fell from her lips slowly, unsure but firm. She let the weight of them sink in, allowing herself a moment to steady her thoughts.

There was a long silence on the other end of the line, and Layla held her breath, the quiet stretching painfully long. Every second felt like an eternity, as if the weight of her decision hung in the air, unspoken, between her and her mother. She could feel the tension in her chest, that knot tightening with each passing moment. It wasn't that she didn't understand her mother's concern—Layla knew it came from a place of love. But it was suffocating, that concern. It pressed down on her, a reminder of all the reasons she had stayed in the past, of all the fears and doubts that had once paralyzed her. But she had pushed through all of that. She had made her choice, and now it was time to own it.

Layla's fingers curled around the edge of the phone, the skin of her palm starting to burn from the pressure. She wasn't sure if it was the heat from the call or the weight of the decision, but she felt like she was suffocating, like her lungs couldn't quite get enough air. The sound of her mother's breath on the other end of the line—slow and deliberate—felt like it was reverberating inside her skull, loud and deafening. It made her stomach twist, reminding her of all the unspoken things between them, the things she wasn't ready to say but had to. She wasn't sure what her mother expected her to say, but Layla knew this moment had already passed the point of no return.

Finally, her mother spoke again, her voice softer now, quieter, as if the weight of her words had somehow settled into the silence between them. "I just want you to be happy, sweetheart. But I can't help but worry. Is this really what you want, or is it just... running away?"

The question hit Layla harder than she expected. It stung. The sting was sharp and quick, like the slice of a blade she hadn't seen coming. Was she running away? Was she fleeing from the mess she had created? Her heart pounded in her chest as the thought spiraled in her mind, making her feel dizzy. She couldn't stay in this place any longer. She couldn't keep pretending that everything was going to fix itself on its own. She had waited for so long for things to change. She had given her all to a life that never quite worked, never quite felt like it was *hers*. Was she running away? Or was she running toward something better? Toward a life, she had promised herself, a life that wasn't dictated by the broken promises of the past?

Layla swallowed hard, forcing the question to the back of her mind. "I'm not running away, Mom," she said quietly, her voice firm this time as if she were trying to convince herself as much as her mother. "I'm running toward a better future—for me, for the kids." The words felt like they came from some distant place inside her, a place she had almost forgotten existed. But she let them slip out, each one holding more weight than the last. "I've spent too long waiting for things to change on their own. I've realized it's up to me to make that change happen."

Her voice cracked slightly as she spoke, but she refused to let herself break. She had come too far and sacrificed too much, and there was no turning back now. The weight of it all—the years of silence, of pretending everything was fine, of waiting for the right time to leave—it all came crashing down in that moment. She could feel the reality of it settling in, like an anchor pulling her deeper into something new. She had to make this work for herself, for Mia, for Noah. She had to believe that it was possible, that she could create a life for them that was better than the one they had left behind.

Her mother's voice softened, and Layla could hear the tears in it now, the emotion breaking through. "You always were the strong one, Layla. Just... don't forget about us, okay?"

The words hit Layla like a ton of bricks. Don't forget about us. The plea rang in her ears, a soft, heartbreaking reminder of how much her mother depended on her. But Layla had to push through. She couldn't stay in this place of broken promises, this place where nothing ever seemed to change.

"Never," Layla promised, her voice a whisper but strong with resolve. "I'll be okay, I promise. Just give me a little time." The words came out more like a prayer than a promise, as though she, too, needed reassurance that everything would work out.

She hung up the phone, her heart pounding in her chest as the finality of the conversation settled in. A mix of guilt and relief coursed through her veins. Guilt for leaving her mother to worry, guilt for walking away from the only life she had ever known. But relief, too, relief that she had finally voiced the decision aloud, that she had said the words that had been stuck in her throat for so long. It was done now. There was no turning back.

She set the phone down on the counter with a soft clink, her hands trembling slightly. She turned back to the room, to the half-packed suitcase that sat on the floor, a tangible reminder of the life she was leaving behind. Clothes, books, toys—everything they could carry—were piled inside haphazardly, but there was still more to do. The reality of the move, of what lay ahead, hadn't quite sunk in yet, and the thought of it made her feel unmoored. She couldn't stay here any longer, but the idea of stepping into the unknown was as terrifying as it was freeing.

As she picked up a pile of clothes from the bed and began to fold them, she let her mind wander back to the life she had once dreamed of before everything had gone wrong. It seemed like a lifetime ago. But as she folded the clothes, one by one, she could still remember the first time she met Jason. He had been everything she thought she needed. Charming, ambitious, full of promise. He had a smile that could melt anyone's heart. She had fallen for him quickly, the way young love often works, swept up in the fantasy of it all.

She had imagined a life built together—of shared dreams and laughter, of raising a family and growing old together. There had been good moments, beautiful moments, even. But somewhere along the way, things started to shift. Layla had seen the warning signs. The late nights at the office, the secretive phone calls, the way he would pull away emotionally, distancing himself. But she had pushed those thoughts aside, convincing herself that their love was strong enough to weather any storm, that they could get through it together.

But she had been wrong.

The betrayal came one evening, just like that. She had stayed up late, waiting for him to come home. He had promised he would be back early, but it was well past midnight when she finally heard the key in the door. She was sitting on the couch, her stomach in knots, when his phone buzzed on the kitchen counter. Without thinking, Layla picked it up. It was a message from a woman she didn't recognize, filled with words that shattered everything she thought she knew about him. She never asked him about it. She didn't need to. The truth was already clear. He wasn't the man she thought he was.

The pain of it had been too much to handle. The wound it left wouldn't heal. Layla had tried to hold their family together, tried to make it work, but eventually, she realized something crucial—she couldn't fix something that was broken beyond repair.

The memories of those nights—the anger, the tears, the silence—flooded back in a rush, making it hard to breathe. The days that followed had felt like a blur of exhaustion and heartbreak, but nothing seemed to shift. Nothing seemed to change.

Layla closed her eyes now, taking a deep breath as she wiped away the unexpected tears. She wasn't sure why they came, but she allowed herself a moment to grieve. She couldn't stay in this place any longer. She couldn't keep pretending that everything would fix itself. She hadn't chosen this ending. She would've fought harder, stayed longer. But you can't build a life with someone who already packed their bags in silence.

With a final glance at the packed suitcase, Layla picked up the last few things she needed, the final remnants of a life she was leaving behind, and zipped it closed. Tomorrow was the day. The future awaited, and there was no turning back now. It wasn't just about moving—it was about reclaiming her life, her peace, and her children's future.

Tomorrow, everything would change.

Chapter 2:

Unraveled

Layla's alarm buzzed loudly, cutting through the silence of the early morning. She had barely slept the night before, her mind racing with the weight of the decision she'd made. The time had come to leave. She glanced over at Mia, still curled up in her blanket, her soft breathing the only sound filling the room. Noah was already awake, his bright eyes wide as he gazed up at her. The long day ahead stretched before her, but for a moment, she allowed herself to feel the weight of the choice she was making. She was leaving the life she had known, for a future she couldn't predict.

With a deep breath, Layla stood up, the floor cold beneath her feet, and began the final preparations. She had already packed the last of their things into two suitcases, each one filled with the hopes of a new life. The house around her, a mix of half-packed boxes and strewn clothes, was a stark reminder of what she was leaving behind. She couldn't look at it for too long—each familiar item seemed to weigh heavier than the last.

Mia stirred in bed, rubbing her eyes as she sat up. "Mom, when are we going to the airport?"

Layla smiled at her daughter, the warmth of her little face calming the knots in her stomach. "Soon, baby. We'll be on a big plane today, okay?"

Mia nodded enthusiastically, her excitement contagious. But Layla's stomach turned. She wasn't sure what to expect once they arrived at the airport, but she knew there was no turning back.

After a hasty breakfast, they loaded into the taxi, the morning sun shining brightly outside. The city that had been home for so long now seemed foreign to her, the streets filled with memories she was ready to leave behind. Memories of Jason—the man she had loved, the father of her children, and the person she had trusted with her heart. But now, those memories only weighed her down. The betrayal, the lies, the emptiness she had felt when their relationship fell

20

apart—it all seemed to linger in the air as she made her way to the airport.

As the taxi drove past familiar streets, Layla's thoughts drifted back to Jason. The days they'd spent together were filled with love, hopes, and shared dreams. Those first months had felt almost magical, as if their lives were perfectly in sync, entwined in ways that felt meant to be. But sometimes, even the most beautiful beginnings don't guarantee forever.

Their disagreements started small—little things like forgotten chores or missed plans. Both Jason and Layla worked long hours, and the exhaustion slowly seeped into their relationship. Tiredness made it harder to communicate, and those small cracks in their connection grew wider over time. Missed dates, unspoken feelings, and misunderstandings piled up, creating distance between them.

It wasn't just about what Jason did or didn't do; Layla knew her own silence and stubbornness played a part, too. She had her own struggles—her own ways of shutting down when things got hard. Their love wasn't failing because one person was at fault; it was because two people who cared deeply didn't know how to hold on in the way the other needed.

Then came the moment that changed everything. Layla found messages on Jason's phone—messages from someone else. It was painful, yes, but it wasn't the end of their story in bitterness or anger. She confronted Jason, trying to understand what had happened between them. But the truth was clear: Jason's feelings had shifted, and despite the love that still lingered between them, the relationship wasn't reciprocal anymore.

Now, as Layla sat in the back of the taxi, the weight of heartbreak was heavy, but it was tempered by something else—a quiet acceptance. She realized she was leaving not out of anger or bitterness but because she still loved him and because she knew their love, as much as it once was, wasn't enough to keep them together. She was leaving with hope—hope for herself, for Mia and Noah, and for a future where love was mutual and healing was possible. This was her chance to find peace on her own terms.

The taxi pulled into the airport, and Layla took a deep breath. It was time.

Inside the terminal, the bustling crowd seemed endless, and Layla clutched Mia's hand tightly while Noah rested against her chest. They moved through the crowded lines to check in, her heart pounding in her chest. It was a strange feeling. She wasn't sure what awaited her once she stepped onto that plane, but she knew she couldn't stay where she was any longer. She was leaving behind a life built on lies, but she was also leaving behind the possibility of starting fresh, of finding a way to make things right for her children and herself.

Once through security, Layla and her children made their way to the gate. She sat down, trying to comfort Noah as he began to fidget in her arms. Mia was already asking questions about the plane, her excitement filling the space between them. The flight was a new chapter, but her thoughts kept drifting back to the past. She couldn't help but think of Jason. There were still so many emotions—anger, hurt, and even love. She hadn't stopped loving him, even though she knew it was over. How could she stop loving someone who had once been everything to her?

As the time to board neared, Layla stood up, taking Mia's hand and securing Noah in the carrier. She walked to the gate, her mind racing. *This is it. This is the start of something new.*

It was a small but significant step—boarding that plane, walking into the unknown, and leaving behind the pieces of her broken past.

The hum of the plane's engines filled the air as Layla sat back in her seat, her gaze fixed on the small window beside her. The world outside was a blur of clouds and endless blue, as though the sky itself was embracing her decision to leave. She had no idea where this journey would take her, but there was something undeniably freeing about the thought of starting fresh.

Mia sat beside her, her small head pressed against Layla's shoulder, already asleep after a long day of travel. Noah was cradled in her arms, his tiny fingers wrapped around her finger as he drifted off to sleep, too. Layla smiled softly, feeling the warmth of her children, her two little anchors in the chaos of her life. They were her reason for everything. As the plane ascended into the unknown, Layla let out a breath she didn't realize she'd been holding. The decision had been made. There was no turning back now.

The weight of the past few days, the packing, the farewells, the uncertainty, all felt distant now, almost like a bad dream. The plane's steady ascent carried her away from it all. She let herself relax for a moment, her body adjusting to the rhythmic motion of the plane. It was a strange feeling, knowing that everything she had once known was now behind her. No more late-night arguments, no more trying to make sense of a relationship that never truly fit. No more pretending everything was okay when it wasn't.

As she felt a burden being lifted from her shoulders, she couldn't help but think about the life that had led her to this point. The memories rushed in, unbidden but inevitable. Her mind drifted back to the streets of her childhood—the place she had once called home.

Layla was just a little girl when she first became aware of the world around her—the harshness of the streets, the unspoken rules of survival in their gritty, crime-ridden neighborhood in New York City. Sirens were a constant soundtrack, wailing through the night like a lullaby for the troubled. Layla had grown used to the sound of gunshots in the distance, the shrill crack of glass breaking, and the tense murmur of the adults around her, trying to pretend everything was fine, even when it clearly wasn't.

Her childhood was framed by these sounds—these daily reminders that the world outside their small apartment wasn't safe. The corner store, just a block away, was a place of fleeting comfort. The same street she played on by day was where the danger lurked after dark. Her mother, Eva, always told her to be careful, but the warning sounded more like a habit than an actual concern, a resigned tone that came with living in a place where danger was a part of life.

Layla's father, Alex, had been absent for as long as she could remember, a shadow that lingered in the background of her early life. He had left when she was barely old enough to understand what it meant to be abandoned, and his absence had shaped her perception of what it meant to be loved. Layla didn't miss him—she didn't know him well enough to miss him—but there was always an emptiness in her heart, a gap she could never quite fill.

Her mother, Eva, did her best to create a stable home, but the pressure of doing it alone weighed heavily on her. Eva worked long hours as a nurse, leaving Layla to fend for herself for much of the day. But it wasn't just the long hours that strained Eva's spirit—it was the constant pressure of their environment. Brooklyn was a place where survival was a daily struggle, where the danger lurking on the corners wasn't just an afterthought—it was an inescapable reality.

In place of her biological father, her stepfather, Jack, had come into her life. Eva had gotten remarried to Jack when Layla was six years old. Jack wasn't perfect. He didn't sweep them away from their circumstances or provide the fairy tale Layla had once imagined. But he was there. His love for her mother, Eva, was evident in the quiet ways he showed up every day, even when things weren't easy.

The apartment was small, and the air felt thick with the struggle to survive. Layla had learned early on that there were no easy answers to the problems they faced, no clean solutions to their lives. But despite it all, she knew there was love between her mother and stepfather. Their relationship, though imperfect, was built on something deeper than the chaos that surrounded them. They didn't always get along, and there were times when Jack seemed lost in his own battles, but Layla always knew, even as a child, that he loved her and her mother in his own way.

But it wasn't always easy. There were moments when Jack's struggles—his personal demons—felt larger than anything Layla could understand. The moments of tension, the times he seemed distant, were not lost on her. She learned that love didn't always look like the perfect image she had once imagined.

Sometimes, it was simply about showing up, day after day, even when things weren't going well.

One night, when Layla was about twelve, she came home late from a friend's house and found Eva and Jack in the middle of a quiet but tense argument. Layla stood in the doorway, unsure whether to enter, but the conversation between her mother and Jack caught her attention.

"I'm trying, Eva," Jack said softly, his voice carrying more exhaustion than anger. He leaned against the counter, his hands gripping the edge like he was holding on to something.

Eva, looking tired, stood with her arms crossed. "I know you're trying, but it feels like we're always barely getting by. You're working long hours, and I'm working long hours, and we're just..." She paused, searching for the right words. "We're just so stretched thin. I don't know what to do anymore."

Layla, standing silently, could feel the weight of the moment—her mother, normally so strong and composed, sounded so vulnerable. Jack's face softened as he looked at her mother, his posture relaxing.

"We're doing the best we can, Eva," he said quietly, as if trying to convince himself. "I know it's not perfect. But we'll make it work, just like we always do."

Eva sighed, her frustration still evident but tempered by Jack's words. "I just... I don't want to keep scraping by. I want more for you, for Layla. I want more for all of us."

Layla, standing in the shadows of the kitchen, realized something then. Her parents' love wasn't perfect. It wasn't easy or simple. But it was real. It wasn't always smooth sailing, and it wasn't always easy to see through the struggles. But through it all, she could see that both Jack and Eva tried. They tried to make it work, tried to love each other even when things weren't ideal. And in that moment, Layla understood that love wasn't perfect. It wasn't always grand or flawless, but it was there, in the little things.

Her mother and Jack weren't perfect, but they had given Layla something more valuable than the idea of perfection: the understanding that love, though messy and flawed, was worth fighting for. This lesson, though subtle, stayed with Layla throughout her life.

Chapter 3:

A Good Enough Goodbye

As she grew older, Layla held onto that lesson tightly, even as she faced her own struggles with love and relationships. It wasn't lost on her that the picture she'd held of what love should be was painted by imperfect hands. She learned early on that love required more than feelings—it demanded patience, understanding, and the willingness to grow alongside another person.

Layla first met Jason back in high school. He wasn't the loudest or most outgoing boy in their class, but there was something about him that quietly stood out—a calm presence amid the teenage chaos. She liked him a lot then, though their interactions were few and far between: a shared glance in the hallway, the way he listened more than he spoke, his easy smile that seemed to hold more than he let on. They weren't close, not yet, but even in those fleeting moments, Layla felt a spark—a feeling that lingered in the background of her memories.

Life, as it often does, pulled them apart after graduation. They went their separate ways, each chasing dreams and navigating the messy, uncertain roads of early adulthood. Years passed, filled with their own struggles, heartbreaks, and growth. But the memory of Jason—the quiet boy with the kind eyes—never completely faded.

Then, one rainy afternoon, long after high school had become a distant chapter, fate brought them back together. It wasn't a movie-perfect reunion, just a chance meeting in a small café tucked away from the noise and rush of the city streets. Jason's smile that day was quiet and easy, like it had simply been waiting there for her all along. There was a softness in his eyes, a steadiness that made her feel safe—like a steady rock in the unpredictable tide of her life.

That day, they talked like old friends who somehow found their way back to each other. The familiarity was comforting but new, layered with all the years and experiences they'd each carried alone. For Layla, it felt like a second chance—not just at love, but at building something real, something lasting.

Those first few months were full of simple moments—coffee shared between shifts, quick dinners after long days, laughter that felt good but didn't need to be perfect. They talked about the future in practical terms: jobs, rent, saving for a place of their own. Jason remembered the small things— how Layla liked her coffee, the songs she hummed while cooking, the way she tucked her hair behind her ear when she was nervous. When things got tough or uncertain, he was there, squeezing her hand, reminding her she wasn't alone.

They made plans, not the kind that felt like fairy tales, but the kind that spoke to real life—raising kids, paying bills, carving out a space where their family could grow. It was messy and complicated, but it was theirs. On paper, they looked like the kind of couple who had it together—young, hopeful, and trying to build something lasting.

Then their children came—Mia first, an easy, content baby who arrived during a time when their family felt relatively steady and hopeful. Layla remembered those early days with a quiet fondness—the gentle rhythm of Mia's breathing at night, the way her soft coos would bring a moment of peace after long, tiring days. Holding her tiny daughter for the first time, Layla felt a surge of overwhelming love and responsibility, unlike anything she had known. Mia's calm presence seemed to soothe the chaos of their lives, offering a steady anchor as they navigated the early challenges of parenthood.

But a few years later, everything changed again with the arrival of Noah. His birth was a harder, more painful journey, coming at a time when the pressures of life weighed heavier than before. Noah was the wild, spirited child—full of energy, fearless, and unpredictable. His arrival brought a whirlwind of activity and noise into their home, stretching Layla in new ways. The house buzzed with his laughter and his endless motion, and while exhausting, his fierce vitality reminded Layla of the strength and resilience she carried within herself.

Motherhood changed everything. It deepened Layla's feelings for Jason but also showed her the cracks they'd been ignoring. They were building a life together, but it wasn't always easy. Long days and longer nights wore them down. Layla often came home exhausted, juggling the demands of work and children, while Jason's job took him away for hours on end. The conversations grew shorter, the silences stretched longer, and the weight of unspoken frustrations settled between them.

Small irritations—forgotten groceries, missed calls, quiet withdrawals—started piling up. Layla's own stubbornness made her close off when she should have spoken up, and Jason's growing distance left her feeling isolated. Neither of them said what might have helped, and slowly, their connection frayed.

Their love didn't disappear—it became quieter, more complicated. Both held onto what they could, but neither knew how to fix what was breaking.

Then, came the day Layla found messages on Jason's phone, and then everything changed; their story— once full of hope—was becoming two lives drifting apart, even as they still cared.

The hurt was sharp, but the realization was clearer still. Layla knew she wasn't blameless. Her silence, her walls, and the things left unsaid had played their part. Jason had his own faults. Their love, real as it was, had simply become unbalanced.

Walking away wasn't about anger or bitterness. It was about love—the kind of love that knows when holding on does more harm than good. For herself, for Mia, for Noah, Layla chose to stop waiting for a love that wasn't there anymore and to start carving out a new path on her own terms.

But even with that clarity, the weight of what lay ahead pressed heavily on her. The nights grew long, filled with restless thoughts and doubts about what the future might hold. One evening, after a particularly exhausting day, Layla sank onto her couch, her mind swirling with exhaustion and uncertainty.

Her phone buzzed softly beside her—a small vibration cutting through the quiet room. She glanced down to see a message from Ashley, her oldest friend, who had moved years ago to a small island far removed from the constant noise and chaos of the city. The message felt like a gentle nudge, a lifeline reaching across the miles.

"Hey, Layla. You've been quiet lately. Everything alright?"

Layla stared at the screen for a long moment, the question echoing in her mind. Was everything alright? Could she even begin to explain the storm inside her? She hesitated, fingers hovering above the keyboard, unsure if she was ready to open up. Then, finally, she typed: "Just tired, I guess. Thinking a lot."

Almost immediately, Ashley replied, her words warm and familiar: "I get that. Sometimes, a change of scene can help clear your head. You ever thought about coming here? I might be able to help you find something to do. It's not paradise, but it's a fresh start."

Layla felt a flicker of something she hadn't felt in a long time—hope. But it was tangled with doubt, fear, and a deep uncertainty about leaving everything she knew behind. The city, her kids' school, the familiar streets, and even the memory of Jason—all of it weighed heavily on her heart.

She typed slowly, almost as if testing the waters: "I don't know if I'm ready for that. It's a big step, Ashley. The kids, the job, everything. I'm scared it won't work."

Ashley's reply was quick, honest, and free of any false promises: "I get it. I was scared, too, when I first came here. But sometimes, staying stuck hurts more than the jump. I work at a company here—not a huge business, but stable. They're looking for someone reliable. If you want, I can put in a good word for you."

Layla stared at the message, her mind a swirl of terror and excitement. Starting over seemed like walking into the unknown, but Ashley's words made it feel a little less daunting.

"Tell me more about the job," she typed, her fingers trembling just slightly.

Ashley explained patiently: "It's an entry-level position at a company that focuses on community projects and tourism development. It's manageable, not glamorous, but honest work with room to grow. It's the kind of job that can help you build a foundation for your family."

Layla imagined the island, the new life Ashley described. It wasn't a fairy tale—it was real, with its own challenges and rewards.

Ashley added quietly, "It's not a magic fix. But it's steady. And I'll help you settle in. I know the ropes."

The weight of the decision pressed heavily on Layla's chest. She hesitated, then typed, "I'm scared, but maybe it's time. For me, for the kids."

Over the next few days, their messages back and forth became a thread of hope in Layla's tangled thoughts. Ashley answered every question patiently, never promising easy days, only steady support. Layla shared her fears and dreams, feeling the fragile hope grow with every exchange.

Then, one afternoon, Ashley's message appeared, simple but powerful: "The position's still open. If you want, I can introduce you to the manager. It could be your first step."

Layla stared at the screen, the fragile thread of hope tightening in her chest. It wasn't perfect. It wasn't a dream. But it was a chance. And sometimes, that's all you need…

Lost in her thoughts, the memories and emotions of the past weeks and years swirled around her like a distant storm, pulling her deep into reflection.

Then, the gentle but firm voice of the captain cut through the haze, crisp and clear over the cabin speakers.

"Ladies and gentlemen, we will be landing shortly. Please fasten your seatbelts and prepare for arrival."

The announcement pulled Layla abruptly from the depths of her memories. Her eyes fluttered open, and for a moment, the hum of the engines and the soft murmur of fellow passengers filled her senses. The island below was no longer a distant hope but a tangible reality growing ever closer.

She took a deep breath, the present moment grounding her as the plane began its final approach. She squeezed Mia's hand gently, held Noah a little closer, and let herself feel the weight of the past slowly lifting—replaced by the quiet promise of what lay ahead.

She took a deep breath, the present moment grounding her as the plane began its final approach. She squeezed Mia's hand gently, held Noah a little closer, and took a deep breath. The weight of the past slowly lifted, replaced by the quiet promise of what lay ahead.

This was her beginning.

Chapter 4:

Where the Quiet Lives

The warm island sun filtered through the plane's small window as it touched down, the wheels gently meeting the runway with a soft thud. Layla's heart pounded with a mix of relief and excitement, a nervous energy coursing through her veins. This was it. A fresh start—not just a dream anymore, but a tangible place she could call home, a place where she could build a new life for Mia, Noah, and herself.

Outside, the sky was streaked with the golden hues of late afternoon, the light casting a honeyed glow across the runway and the low buildings clustered nearby. The air shimmered faintly with heat and humidity, carrying the scent of salt, wild hibiscus, and tropical pine mingling in the breeze. As the plane slowed, Layla felt a flutter in her stomach—a blend of hope and uncertainty.

She gathered her things slowly, careful not to jostle Noah asleep in her arms. Mia's small hand was warm and steady in hers, the grip both grounding and fragile at once. They moved through the plane's aisle, every step carrying Layla closer to a new chapter, yet farther from everything she knew.

Stepping off into the humid air, Layla inhaled deeply. The island's landscape was a painter's palette of emerald-green palms, vibrant bougainvillea cascading over rustic fences, and narrow cobblestone streets lined with pastel-colored cottages whose shutters creaked softly in the warm breeze. Sounds floated through the air—the distant rhythm of waves crashing, the low hum of island life, voices laced with unfamiliar accents, and the soft chatter of other travelers.

The sun hung low, beginning its slow descent behind palm trees swaying gently in the breeze. The island streets below buzzed with a slower, gentler rhythm than the relentless city pulse she had left behind. Brightly painted buildings stood shoulder to shoulder, their colors vivid and sunbaked, and narrow sidewalks bustled with locals moving with relaxed purpose.

Holding Noah close, Layla felt the knot of excitement and fear tighten in her chest. The reality of this place, its beauty, and its strangeness, settled over her like a heavy blanket. For months, Ashley's messages had been a fragile thread pulling her toward this new life—promises of opportunity and renewal. But now, here, the unknown stretched before her like an uncharted sea.

Ashley waited for them at the small airport café—a familiar face amid the unfamiliar crowd. Her smile was quick but tired, eyes flickering with sympathy as she wrapped Layla and the children in a warm hug. Ashley had been Layla's steady friend through months of phone calls and messages, a lifeline in the distance.

"I'm so glad you made it," Ashley said softly, squeezing Layla's arm gently. "I've been counting down the days."

Layla managed a smile, but inside, the tightness of uncertainty refused to loosen. Over the next few hours, they walked through the bustling island streets, Ashley pointing out places to buy groceries, schools for the kids, and the office where she worked. The island thrummed with life—vibrant colors, unfamiliar sounds, smells that teased the senses—all new and a little overwhelming.

The narrow streets were alive with the hum of scooters and the chatter of market vendors, and children darted between stalls selling fresh fruit, woven baskets, and brightly dyed textiles. The air was thick with the scent of roasting coffee beans and grilled seafood, occasionally interrupted by the sharp tang of sea salt carried on the breeze. For a moment, Layla let herself soak in the scene—a different world, but a world she had to learn to call home.

That evening, the three of them sat in Ashley's modest apartment. A single lamp cast a soft glow over a cluttered kitchen table strewn with papers and half-empty mugs. Ashley had promised Layla a role at the company she worked for—a small but steady firm involved in community projects and tourism development. It wasn't a glamorous promise, but it was a start, a foothold.

But as Ashley's words spilled out, Layla's hope began to fracture.

"Layla, I need to be honest with you," Ashley said carefully, fingers nervously tracing the rim of her coffee cup. "The position I told you about... It's no longer available. The company's restructuring and they had to put hiring on hold. I just found out today."

Layla was silent for a long moment, the weight of the news settling like a stone in her stomach. She had left everything behind based on this promise—the city, her life, her children's routine—and now it felt like the ground had shifted beneath her feet.

"But... I thought it was solid," Layla whispered, her voice fragile.

"I know," Ashley said softly, eyes downcast. "I'm sorry. I wish I had better news."

Layla swallowed hard, blinking back the sudden sting of tears. She looked down at Noah, who played quietly with a toy car, and then at Mia, who was tracing shapes on a notepad. Their futures suddenly felt more precarious than ever.

"I put everything on this," Layla admitted, voice cracking. "The move, the kids, leaving my family and Jason... I didn't have a backup plan."

Ashley reached out, squeezing Layla's hand. "You're not alone. We'll figure it out—together. This isn't the end."

Despite Ashley's words, the nights that followed were long and filled with doubt. Layla lay awake in the dark, the moonlight casting silver shadows on the walls. Fear and uncertainty gnawed at her, and for the first time since she'd made the decision to move, she began to question whether she'd made the right choice. She had left behind everything she knew— her familiar routine, her friends, her family, and even the painful but familiar existence she had lived with Jason.

In the stillness of the night, those thoughts swirled like a storm. Was she being reckless? Had she dragged Mia and Noah to a place where they would struggle just as much, if not more than they had before? The promise of a fresh start felt like a fragile illusion. Was she selfish for hoping for something better? Could she really build a life here?

For the first time, Layla questioned whether she'd made a huge mistake. The weight of her decision, the unknowns stretching before her like an endless road, seemed impossible to navigate. She missed the ease of the life they had back home, even though it had been far from perfect. She longed for the comfort of knowing what each day would bring. Now, every choice felt like a risk, and she was afraid she had bet everything on an uncertain future.

But as the silence of the night wrapped around her, Layla could almost hear her mother's voice in the back of her mind—the one that had always told her to keep moving, to never let fear hold her back for too long. She thought about Mia and Noah, their innocent faces, and the future she wanted to give them. She couldn't afford to second-guess herself now. If she didn't take action, if she didn't push through the doubt, they would have nothing.

The next morning, after a restless night filled with too many "what ifs," Layla woke up with a renewed sense of determination. It wasn't much, but it was enough to get her feet moving. She couldn't let the uncertainty of the island become a reason to retreat. She had to start somewhere. Slowly, she stood up, wiped the sleep from her eyes, and pushed aside the nagging fear that threatened to hold her back.

Within a few days, Layla had sent out several applications for part-time jobs. She applied to cafés, local stores, and even a small boutique on the beach. Anything that would give her a sense of stability. The work wasn't glamorous, but it was something she could do, something that would help support her children while she figured out the next steps.

Even as she typed the words into her application forms, she felt a mixture of skepticism and resolve. Was she doing the right thing? Could this be the beginning of something, or was she simply treading water?

But by the end of the week, she had received a call back from a small café down the road, offering her a part-time position. The work was tiring, the pay modest, but it was a start—more than she had hoped for. It wasn't a dream job, but it was hers. Each day was a delicate juggling act—caring for Mia and Noah, navigating the demands of her job, and wrestling with the gnawing anxiety of the unknown.

Yet, every night after the children were asleep, Layla carved out moments for herself at the small kitchen table. She pulled out her worn notebook and began to scribble—ideas, sketches, dreams of a business she could call her own. Drawing on years of experience, she looked for gaps in the community she could fill. She imagined a venture built by her own hands, independent of broken promises and shaky opportunities.

Some nights, the loneliness pressed down hard. She missed the steady pulse of city life, the comfort of old friends, and even the complicated love she had left behind. But those feelings fueled her determination.

"I won't let this break me," she whispered into the quiet.

Slowly, Layla began to reach out—talking to local shopkeepers, market vendors, anyone who might listen. She nervously pitched her ideas, collected feedback, and adjusted her plans. The process was daunting. She stumbled over words, felt the sting of polite rejections, but each conversation pushed her forward.

One afternoon, sitting on the sun-warmed sand, notebook open in her lap, Layla watched Mia and Noah play nearby. Their laughter mingled with the gentle crash of the waves. In that moment, the weight she'd carried felt lighter.

She realized this was no longer just survival. This was about building. Building a future on her own terms.

Closing the notebook, Layla gazed out at the endless horizon, the vast ocean stretching before her. The possibilities felt as wide as the water itself.

This was no longer a fresh start.

This was her beginning.

Chapter 5:

All the Things I Didn't Say

Layla stood alone on the island, the soft, salty breeze brushing against her skin like a tender caress. The rhythmic crash of the waves against the shore was the only sound that filled the air, each wave breaking with the same steady force, as if time itself were moving in an unyielding cycle. She gazed out at the vast horizon, where the sky and ocean met in an endless embrace. The view was stunning, picturesque even—this place, the one she had come to, was supposed to offer a fresh start, a new chapter. But as she stood there, alone, staring into the infinity before her, a deep unease settled in her chest.

This wasn't the adventure she had hoped for, the one where the universe would sweep her away into something bold, something that promised a reinvention of herself. No, what she felt was nothing like that. It was more like the fading echo of a promise that had never quite materialized. There was no sweeping change waiting for her. No magical transformation. What had brought her here wasn't the promise of a new life—it was the raw, undeniable need to survive. Survival, not escape, had led her here. And as she stood by the ocean, her feet buried in the sand, the harsh truth settled like a weight in her stomach. This wasn't the beginning of something new—it was just the next step. The one she had to take, because she had no choice but to move forward.

By the time Layla stepped onto that plane, nearly two years had passed since he left. She hadn't left him— no, she never would have. Those words seemed to echo in her mind, repeating like a mantra, trying to make sense of what had happened. Sitting there on the island, watching the way the sky dipped into the sea, she couldn't help but feel as though her heart was still caught somewhere in the past. It was as though a part of her was stuck in time, unable to catch up with the life she was now living. She was physically here, but emotionally? She wasn't sure where she was. Her thoughts scattered in all directions, fractured pieces of a puzzle she could no longer fit together. The pieces didn't make sense anymore. She wasn't sure she even wanted them to.

She hadn't chosen this path. It wasn't a conscious decision to throw her life into turmoil—it was simply a twist of fate, an event beyond her control that had reshaped her world. There was no grand plan, no brave leap forward into the unknown. The move wasn't about finding herself. It wasn't an escape; it was just survival. The kind of survival that meant distancing herself from a past that had been ripped away without warning. She didn't have the luxury of time to prepare, to process. One moment, everything seemed like it was going to work out, and the next, everything she had known was gone. No explanation. No reason. Just an absence, a silence, and a painful ache that wouldn't go away.

Layla never had the chance to choose to leave him. She didn't even get the chance to make the decision. One day, he was simply gone. There was no goodbye. No last conversation. It was as if the universe had decided for her, pulling him away without so much as a whisper of warning. The void he left behind was like being tossed into a storm— only to realize the storm was not outside of her, but inside. Her world didn't collapse in one dramatic moment; there was no climactic unraveling of emotions. It wasn't like the movies. There was no final confrontation or cathartic release. Instead, there was just the aftermath—the quiet aftermath that felt like it might swallow her whole. The silence was deafening. And with that silence came the painful realization that while life had continued its march forward, she had stayed frozen, caught in the wreckage of what had been.

The true breaking came after he left, in the long, empty days that followed. The initial shock of his departure had been sharp, cutting deep like a wound that didn't yet know how to bleed. But it wasn't the immediate pain that lingered the most. It was the hollow days that followed—the days that stretched on like an endless blur. It was the quiet house that echoed with the sound of emptiness, the empty mornings when she woke alone, the space beside her in the bed where his warmth used to be. There was no one to share the small moments with, no one to laugh with, no one to argue with, no one to lean on. It was just the empty space, the ghost of what once was, and the overwhelming silence that consumed her. It felt like living in a world that had forgotten her, a world that had kept moving, while she stayed stuck, caught between the past and the future, never fully able to enter either.

She wandered the house like a ghost, moving aimlessly through the rooms that once buzzed with laughter and warmth, now shrouded in silence. The walls, which had once held the echoes of shared moments, seemed to close in on her, the emptiness pressing against her chest. The house felt too large now, too open, as if it had somehow expanded to match the cavernous hollowness inside her. She didn't belong here anymore. The rooms, once vibrant with life, had grown just as desolate as her heart. The place had become a shell, an echo of what was once beautiful, now left to rot in stillness. It felt like the house was mirroring her own sense of loss, growing more empty with each passing day.

Mornings were the hardest. She would wake up, her eyes struggling to adjust to the quiet, and there was no "good morning" waiting for her. No warm hand reaching out in the early light, no coffee brewing, no soft shuffle of his feet moving across the floor. For the first few weeks, she didn't know what to do with herself. The silence was suffocating, a constant companion she couldn't escape from. She busied herself with meaningless tasks—scrubbing the counters, rearranging the furniture, moving things around in an attempt to fill the void. But no matter what she did, the silence clung to everything. It lingered in the air, stuck to the corners of the house, and wrapped itself around her like a heavy cloak. No matter how much she cleaned, how much she tried to make the house feel like a home again, nothing could fill it.

There was no one to text, no one to check in on her anymore. The small, mundane exchanges that had once made up her day were gone, like a world she could no longer access. No one asked how she was doing, no one shared random thoughts or stories. The little things—the "just checking in" messages, the shared inside jokes—had all evaporated, leaving a hollow space in their wake. And when Layla came home at night, there was no "I'm home" to greet her. No familiar scent of him wafting from the kitchen. No warmth waiting for her in the quiet darkness. She was met only by the hollow sound of her own footsteps echoing off the empty walls. She was alone. Completely alone.

The realization hit harder than she expected—that life had moved on without her. The world hadn't stopped to wait for her to catch up. It continued, relentless, as if nothing had changed. The disconnect she felt was suffocating, as if the world was spinning around her, and she was trapped in some distant orbit, unable to connect. She watched the world go on without her, and the further it moved from her, the more disconnected she became. The distance between herself and everything she knew grew wider, until the gap felt insurmountable. She had

been left behind. It wasn't just the absence of him—
it was the absence of everything she once knew. She
couldn't seem to find her place in this new world, a
world that felt colder, harder, less forgiving.

For a while, she tried to play the part of the woman
she used to be—the one who had dreams, the one
who still believed in tomorrow. She tried to be the
person who could go out and find joy again, to find
the things that used to matter. She forced herself to
go through the motions, but it never felt right. The
woman she once was felt like a stranger now,
someone she could barely recognize. Her own skin
felt unfamiliar to her. The body she inhabited didn't
belong to the person she was now—it felt like a
foreign shell, something she had been wearing but
couldn't remove. She didn't know how to exist in this
life, in this new reality that had been thrust upon her.
Everything was cold, unfamiliar, and utterly alien.

Her friends, well-meaning and concerned, tried to
push her out of her shell, encouraging her to "get
back out there," to find someone new, to start over.
They said she deserved happiness, that there was

someone out there who could give her what she needed. But when Layla did try, when she swiped through dating apps, when she forced herself to go out to bars, when she went on a few awkward, hollow dates, it all felt wrong. It wasn't right. It wasn't real. There was no connection, no spark. It was like trying to fit a square peg into a round hole. She wasn't looking for someone new. She wasn't looking for a fresh start. What she wanted was her old life back, the one that had been taken from her without any warning. The life that had slammed the door shut and left her standing outside, unable to return.

For a long time, Layla tried to convince herself that being single could be liberating—that it would give her the chance to rediscover herself, to explore new opportunities, and to grow in ways she hadn't before. She thought that perhaps, in the quiet of her solitude, she could find strength, clarity, and a new sense of purpose. But the reality was far from freeing. It wasn't the self-empowerment she had imagined. It was exhausting. Every day, she felt the weight of an invisible pressure to "move on," to act as though everything was fine when it most certainly wasn't. She kept telling herself that she was okay, that time would heal, that she was strong enough to get through this. But the effort to convince herself only drained her further. The more she forced herself to wear the mask of composure, the more she felt the cracks spreading beneath the surface.

She had become a stranger to herself. The woman she once was, the one full of dreams and hope, felt like a fading memory, and the more she tried to play the part, the further she slipped from who she had been. The mask she wore started to feel heavy, suffocating, and no matter how hard she tried to hold it together, she couldn't shake the feeling that she was losing herself bit by bit. The future she once envisioned— one where Mia and Noah flourished, where they all found joy again—seemed impossibly far away. Those dreams, once so vibrant, now felt like distant stars that she could never quite reach.

One night, after what felt like an eternity of pushing through the motions, Layla sat up in bed, her body exhausted but her mind restless. The house was unnervingly quiet, the kind of stillness that wraps itself around you and makes every breath feel heavy. The shadows outside her window seemed to stretch endlessly, and for the first time in what felt like forever, she didn't feel the need to pretend. There were no expectations, no "shoulds" or "musts" pressing down on her. She wasn't hiding behind any mask of false strength or forced cheerfulness. It was just her and the raw weight of her thoughts. Alone. No distractions. The grief, the confusion, the loss— they all seemed to come crashing down in that moment, overwhelming her until she could barely breathe. She hadn't realized how suffocating it had been to keep pushing forward, to keep pretending she was fine. But now, sitting in that silence, she understood that she couldn't wait for life to start again. It wasn't coming. Life wasn't going to knock on her door and tell her it was time to begin again.

The realization wasn't grand or dramatic. There was no rush of excitement or clarity. No epiphany that would send her running toward a new adventure. It was just a quiet understanding, the kind that settles deep in your bones when you've lived through enough pain to know what you need. It was the kind of survival that doesn't seek glory or recognition. It was a moment of simply seeing things for what they were. Layla realized she could no longer live suspended between the life she had lost and the one she was waiting for. That limbo had become her prison. It wasn't about escaping the past, or chasing after something bigger—it was about finding a way forward. It was about reclaiming her life, piece by piece, even if it meant starting from scratch.

And so, quietly, firmly, Layla made the decision. It wasn't some dramatic turning point. It wasn't about running away or running toward some idealized dream. It was just the understanding that she had no other choice but to move forward. She had to rebuild herself. She had to find a way to live again. And in that moment, there was no hesitation. She knew it wasn't going to be easy. She knew she would stumble and fall, but for the first time in a long while, she felt a spark of determination. It wasn't about pretending to have all the answers—it was about figuring it out, step by step.

By the time Layla moved to the island, the man she had once loved was gone. The life they had built together was gone. But there was one thing that hadn't vanished yet—her. And that's who she had come here to find. Not to escape or to chase some fantasy. She came to the island not to bury the past, but to confront it. She came to figure out how to live again. Because she wasn't sure where she was headed, or what the future might hold, but she knew one thing with certainty: she wasn't just surviving anymore. She was starting to live again. And for now, that was enough.

Chapter 6:

Salt in the Wound

Layla's feet screamed in protest with each step she took as she stumbled toward the back exit of the cafe, her shift finally ending. She'd been standing for hours in the cramped, dimly lit space, her body aching from the strain of being on her feet for so long. The hum of the espresso machines, the constant chatter from the customers, the clink of silverware against plates—it had all become a blur by now. The cafe was small, tucked away in a quiet corner of the island, with a steady stream of regulars and tourists who came in for their coffee, their pastries, and the brief moments of calm they could steal from the chaos of their own lives. Layla had gotten the job a week ago, and while she was grateful, she hadn't anticipated how draining it would be.

The work wasn't bad, not really. It was just... constant. She was always "on." A smile here, a quick conversation there, cleaning tables, refilling cups, repeating it all over and over. Her mind never had a chance to settle, not even for a moment. Serve the customers, clean the counter, pour the coffee, rinse the mugs, repeat.

She had been doing this for two weeks now, and every day felt like she was running on fumes. The exhaustion wasn't just physical—though her legs and back ached from the strain—but mental. She was always thinking, always moving, always *serving*. There was never any time for herself. Even when the customers were pleasant and the tips were decent, Layla couldn't shake the feeling that this wasn't the fresh start she'd hoped for. This wasn't the life she dreamed of when she decided to leave everything behind. This was survival. A never-ending treadmill of obligations.

Her shift felt longer than usual today, each minute dragging by as the customers piled in, their orders never ceasing. The small cafe never quieted, never stopped. She didn't remember the last time she had a real break, and when the final whistle of her shift blew, she just felt... empty. She grabbed her coat with a tired sigh, throwing it over her shoulders like it weighed a hundred pounds, and stepped out the door into the cool, late afternoon air.

As soon as the fresh air hit her face, Layla felt a brief sense of relief, but it was fleeting. She was too tired to process it. The walk to her car felt like a mile, her legs stiff and sore. The reality of what her life had become hit her hard—the never-ending cycle of work, motherhood, and the constant pressure to be more than she was. She had barely had time to breathe, let alone think about whether this life was what she truly wanted.

The grocery store wasn't any better. It was a chore she dreaded with every fiber of her being, but she couldn't avoid it. Her list was small—bread, milk, eggs, fruit—the basics. Simple enough, right? But even the thought of it felt like another mountain to climb. The aisles stretched on forever, the fluorescent lights above buzzing like an insect's drone. Layla couldn't focus. She just walked up and down the aisles, grabbing whatever her brain told her to, but even that was a blur. She could barely keep track of what she had in her cart.

As she moved between the aisles, she noticed how everything looked the same. The same brands, the same boxes of cereal, the same produce. She grabbed a carton of eggs, a loaf of bread, and some milk, but the task felt hollow, a cruel reminder of how much she still hadn't figured out. *This isn't how it's supposed to be,* she thought. *I should have more time. I should be more than just a tired, empty shell of a mother, working at a cafe and trying to make it all work.*

The cashier at the register was friendly, asking how her day had been. Layla tried to smile, but it came out more like a grimace. She nodded absently, swiping her card without much thought. The bag of groceries felt like a small weight in her hands as she loaded it into her car. The drive to pick up Mia and Noah felt like it took forever, her eyes struggling to stay open.

When she finally pulled into the daycare parking lot, the sight of Mia standing by the window, her small face pressed against the glass, hit her like a wave. Layla's heart lurched. Mia was waiting for her, and the guilt hit harder than ever. She should've been there sooner. She should've been able to do more for her. Layla shoved the guilt aside, forcing a smile as she picked Mia up, her little arms immediately wrapping around her neck.

Noah was next, reaching for her with his chubby hands, his face lighting up when he saw her. Layla scooped him up, holding both of them close. For a moment, everything felt right again. For a moment, she could pretend that she wasn't exhausted, that she hadn't just spent the day doing everything she could to get through it. But as she carried them inside, the weight of her fatigue hit her again, a slow, crushing pressure that she couldn't shake.

At home, the dinner routine felt like it was going to break her. The house was a mess—clothes from yesterday were scattered across the floor, toys were piled up in the living room, and the sink was full of

71

dishes that hadn't been done in days. Layla didn't have the energy to pick up the pieces. She just couldn't. She threw the groceries onto the counter and forced herself to get dinner started. The pasta, the simplest thing she could make, went into a pot. The heat from the stove felt like it was smothering her.

Her mind raced as the pasta boiled. What was she doing? Was this really the life she wanted? Every moment felt stretched so thin. The kids needed her, the house needed her, and she was just running on fumes. She didn't know how to fix any of it.

When she finally set the food on the table, she felt a wave of dread. Mia took one look at the pasta and pushed it away, frowning. "I don't want this," she said, crossing her arms. Layla's hands tightened on the edge of the table, but she forced herself to stay calm. She told Mia to please just eat, and that they didn't have time for this.

But then Noah, not far behind, started throwing his food on the floor, screaming in protest. Layla felt a rush of heat flood her chest. *Why can't they just eat?* she thought. *Why can't I just get this one thing right?*

Her heart was racing now, the noise escalating, the chaos building. She tried to keep her voice steady, tried to keep calm as she told them to stop. But the frustration, the sheer exhaustion, began to break her. She had done everything. Everything she could. And still, it wasn't enough.

She could feel her resolve cracking. The kids were screaming, the food was wasted, and Layla felt like she was about to lose it, right there in the kitchen. *I'm trying so damn hard,* she thought. *Why can't anything ever just go right?*

She stood frozen for a moment, hands shaking, her breath coming in short gasps. She looked at the mess—the food on the floor, the tantrums, the demands—and everything she was carrying. This life, this overwhelming, relentless life, was crushing her.

Feeling exhausted and frustrated, she turned, walked out of the kitchen, and locked herself in the bathroom. She could still hear the noise, the chaos, but in the small space, she finally let the tears come. The tears came without warning, hot and furious as if her body had finally given up on holding them back. She pressed the towel to her face, muffling the sobs, but they came anyway, raw and shaking. In the background, she could hear Mia's voice—loud, demanding, frustrated with the world. Noah's constant babbling followed, his little hands banging on the walls, wanting her attention, needing her in ways that felt like nails scraping down her skin.

"Fuck, I can't do this anymore," Layla muttered into the towel, her words barely audible beneath the sound of her own breakdown. She slid down the bathroom door, the cool tile against her legs doing nothing to soothe the heat rising in her chest. The room was suffocating; every breath she took felt like it was being stolen. The pressure, the exhaustion, the constant push to be everything to everyone—it was crushing.

"I fucking hate this," she whispered, her voice thick with defeat. "I didn't sign up for this shit."

The thoughts spiraled faster, sharper, jabbing into her mind like a thousand knives. She wanted to scream, to rage, to throw her fist through the door. The constant responsibility of motherhood—alone, without help, without anyone who understood what it was like to be her. The loneliness wrapped itself around her like a wet blanket. The weight of it—of the kids, the responsibilities, the constant decisions, the endless requests—felt heavier by the minute.

"I didn't want to be a fucking nanny. I wanted a fucking partner," she thought, the bitterness licking at the back of her throat. But that was the thing, wasn't it? Layla had once had a partner, but somewhere along the way, things had changed. The connection they had shared had faded, leaving her feeling like she was carrying the weight of the world on her shoulders. Now, after everything she'd left behind, she found herself trapped in the role of a single mother, with no relief in sight. No one to help carry the load. No one to share the burden. Just her and the weight of her own silent breakdowns.

The sobs didn't stop, and neither did the overwhelming sense of rage. Layla gripped the towel harder as if the fabric could absorb all the anger she couldn't release. She wanted to yell at God, wanted to scream at the sky. Why had He given her this life? Why this responsibility, this loneliness, this fucking chaos? She'd prayed for clarity, for peace, for some sign that she was doing the right thing. But all she got in return was silence.

"God, why the fuck did You give me this life if You won't help?" Her words were ugly, desperate. She didn't care. She was past caring. All she had now was the frustration bubbling over, crashing against the walls of her soul. And yet, there was no answer, just the hum of the air conditioning in the next room, the faint noise of her children's voices, and the suffocating silence that seemed to scream back at her.

For a moment, she let the tears come harder, let them pour out until her face was blotchy and raw, until she thought she might drown in her own rage. She didn't care that it was messy, didn't care that she was supposed to be strong. She didn't want to be strong anymore. She wanted to collapse, to be held, to rest.

But she knew she couldn't because she was all she had. She had to keep going. She had to wipe her face, stand up, and pretend everything was okay, pretend that she was okay.

So, after a few more seconds of pure, ugly sobbing, Layla wiped her face roughly with the towel. She glanced at herself in the bathroom mirror, eyes bloodshot and red, hair a tangled mess. She barely recognized the woman staring back at her. But she didn't have time to wallow in self-pity. She had two kids in the other room, both needing her. Both, relying on her.

With a shaky breath, she opened the bathroom door. The noise from the living room hit her like a slap in the face. Mia was still shouting, and Noah was crying. Layla took another breath, wiping away the last remnants of tears, and pasted a smile on her face. She had to fake it. She had no choice.

First, she picked Noah up and made him stop crying, then went into the kitchen, still feeling like a raw, exposed nerve. Mia stopped screaming for a second when she saw her mother, but it wasn't enough. It wasn't enough to quiet the storm inside. She could feel the rage simmering beneath the surface, but she had no outlet for it. No release. Not here. Not now.

Layla set the pan on the stove, the sound of it sizzling loud and sharp in her ears, cutting through the tension. She mixed the pancake batter like it was some kind of ritual—stirring the ingredients together, making something familiar out of all the chaos, trying to force a sense of normalcy onto her broken world. She watched the batter bubble in the pan, trying to focus on the task at hand, forcing herself to do something simple, something that made sense in a world that felt increasingly senseless.

The pancakes weren't perfect. They were a little burnt on the edges, and they stuck to the pan in places. But it didn't matter. Layla didn't need perfect pancakes. She needed something she could control. Something that didn't scream or demand or break her heart. Pancakes were safe. They didn't judge. They didn't ask anything of her except to be made.

As the pancakes cooked, Layla took a deep breath, closed her eyes, and tried to ground herself. She had to be present for her kids, for herself. She couldn't fall apart now. Not yet. Not in front of them.

The pancakes were done, and as she served them to Mia and Noah, Layla smiled, a little smile that cracked across her face like a fragile piece of glass. It wasn't much, but it was enough to make them giggle, enough to make them think she was okay. Enough to make them think that maybe, just maybe, everything would be okay.

But inside, Layla knew. She was still broken. Still angry. Still trying to figure out how to piece it all together.

Chapter 7:

The Blur

The early mornings blurred into late nights, each day folding into the next with a relentless pace. Layla woke before the sun, the soft breathing of Mia and Noah beside her a fragile reminder of why she pushed herself so hard. Her part-time job at the café demanded energy and focus, but it was the nights that tested her will—the quiet hours when the world was still, and she was left alone with her dreams and doubts.

In the small apartment's dim light, Layla spread her notebooks across the worn kitchen table. Pages filled with scribbled ideas, potential contacts, and rough sketches of logos and menus. She had spent days researching, peeling back the layers of the island's economy and culture, looking for a place where her own skills might fit.

It was during one of these late-night sessions, her fingers tracing over a map of the island's resorts and hotels, that an idea began to crystallize. The island was alive with weddings—white-draped tents on sandy beaches, laughter spilling from seaside villas, and elegant corporate retreats that filled calendars months in advance. Yet, beneath the surface, Layla saw a glaring gap. There was no comprehensive event management or catering service to match the demand, no one who could offer the seamless blend of organization, local flavor, and reliability that these events needed.

This was her opening.

Her business could fill that space—not with grand promises or lavish investments, but with authenticity, hard work, and an understanding of what clients truly needed. She pictured herself coordinating celebrations under swaying palms, serving dishes infused with island spices, and crafting moments that would linger in memory long after the guests had gone home.

The thought sparked a fire within her, one that no exhaustion could extinguish.

By day, Layla poured herself into the café, wiping tables, brewing coffee, and balancing orders with a practiced efficiency. The work was physically demanding, her feet aching by evening, but it was a steady income—small but essential. Each tip earned, each smile from a satisfied customer added fuel to her determination.

But by night, the kitchen table transformed into her command center. She reached out to local farmers for fresh ingredients, called small rental companies about tents and chairs, and drafted contracts that could protect both her and her clients. She studied online tutorials about event planning and catering, absorbing everything she could. Slowly, the patchwork of her business began to take shape.

The juggling act was exhausting. Mia's laughter sometimes pulled her from her thoughts, Noah's tired cries sliced through her concentration, and the ever-present anxiety of making ends meet shadowed every moment. Yet, Layla refused to let the weight of it all crush her spirit.

"I won't quit," she whispered to herself on more than one sleepless night. "Not now. Not ever."

Small victories began to take shape. Her first event was a modest birthday party for a local family celebrating their daughter's tenth birthday. It wasn't glamorous, but it was real—something tangible she had built with her own hands. Layla worked tirelessly in the days leading up to it, coordinating with local vendors she had painstakingly met and earned the trust of.

On the morning of the party, she arrived early, greeted by the warm scent of freshly baked cakes mingling with the salty sea air. She meticulously oversaw the table settings, double-checked food deliveries, and handled last-minute requests with a calm determination that surprised even herself.

When the guests arrived, the smiles and laughter filled the small garden, and Layla felt a surge of pride. Her careful planning had paid off. The family thanked her warmly, and a neighbor who attended offered to recommend her services. That first success, small as it was, felt like a lifeline—proof that she could do this.

Several weeks passed before Layla landed her second event—and this one would test her resilience in ways she hadn't anticipated.

It was a corporate retreat for a mid-sized company, held at one of the island's upscale resorts. Layla had secured the gig through a contact she'd met at a local networking event—a few weeks of persistent follow-ups and a well-prepared pitch had finally paid off. This was her chance to prove herself on a larger stage—a moment that felt both thrilling and daunting.

Two days before the retreat, disaster struck.

The catering company she had arranged to provide food unexpectedly canceled. Their main chef had fallen ill, and no substitute could be found on such short notice. Layla's heart sank as she stared at the email on her phone. Panic clawed at her chest. How could she let down her client? How could she fix this in less than forty-eight hours?

The quiet apartment that evening felt suffocating. Noah was asleep in his crib, and Mia lay curled beside her, but Layla couldn't settle. She paced, her mind racing through every possible solution.

Then, a message popped up on her phone. It was from Isabelle, one of her coworkers at the café where she worked. Isabelle had been the first friend Layla made after moving to the island.

"Hey, how's it going? Need some help?"

Layla typed back quickly, explaining the situation in a few hurried sentences.

Within minutes, Isabelle replied: "I know a local chef who runs a small catering business out of her home. She's talented and reliable, but small-scale. I can call her first thing in the morning."

Hope flickered.

The next morning, Isabelle's call came with good news—the chef was available and willing to take on the job on short notice. Layla arranged a meeting that afternoon. She met with the chef, a woman named Marissa, whose warm smile and confident hands inspired immediate trust. They discussed menus, special dietary requests, and logistics late into the evening.

But the challenges didn't end there.

On the day of the retreat, a sudden tropical rainstorm threatened to derail the outdoor setup. Tables and decorations needed to be moved quickly, guests were arriving earlier than expected, and Layla's nerves frayed. Yet, she refused to let panic win.

Drawing on every lesson learned and every connection made, Layla rallied her small team— including Marissa and a few helpful locals she'd hired for setup—and orchestrated a last-minute move indoors. She improvised decorations with vibrant local fabrics, creating a cozy, festive atmosphere that guests admired.

By the time the rain eased, the retreat was in full swing. The clients praised the food, the smooth transitions, and the warm hospitality. Layla breathed deeply for the first time in days, a smile breaking through her exhaustion.

That night, as she sent a heartfelt thank-you message to Isabelle, Layla felt a quiet affirmation settle in her heart: she was building something real. Not just a business but a testament to resilience, creativity, and the power of community

Each success was a thread weaving a fragile safety net beneath her feet. But alongside those moments of hope were the harsh realities: the pay from the café barely covered rent and groceries, the late nights left her bleary-eyed and weary, and the responsibility of building something from scratch weighed heavily on her shoulders. There were times when the loneliness and exhaustion threatened to overwhelm her, when the ghost of past mistakes whispered doubts in the dark.

In those moments, Layla often found herself reflecting on her relationship with Jason—not in bitterness or anger, but with hard-earned clarity. She saw now that the struggle hadn't been about him alone but about the way she had believed she needed to bend and change to be enough. Her walls, her silences, the things left unsaid—they had all played their part. She recognized that the real battle was with her own self-doubt and the fear that she might never be enough on her own.

But this was different. This time, the fight was hers to win.

As the weeks passed, Layla's business began to show signs of life. The inquiries increased, her reputation slowly grew, and she dared to imagine a future where she could provide stability and joy for her children without sacrificing her own dreams. She pictured a small team, a calendar filled with bookings, and a life where her work was her own.

One evening, as the island's sun dipped below the horizon, painting the sky with shades of pink and gold, Layla sat on the small porch of their apartment. Mia and Noah played nearby, their laughter a soothing balm. She opened her notebook, now filled with detailed plans and contacts, and allowed herself to dream—not just of survival but of thriving.

This was no longer just about starting over.

This was about building something real.

Something hers.

Chapter 8:
The Mom Group

Layla wiped down the last table from the morning rush, her hand methodically moving the cloth in small circles over the worn wooden surface, the faint aroma of freshly ground coffee and baked goods lingering around her. She straightened and glanced around the café, feeling a quiet pride in the peaceful scene unfolding. The gentle hum of conversations mixed with the subtle hiss of the espresso machine created a comforting ambiance that she'd grown surprisingly attached to.

Across the room, Isabelle effortlessly chatted with a couple of regulars, her laughter ringing lightly as she took their orders with that easy charm Layla always admired. Isabelle had been working at the café longer and had become someone Layla genuinely enjoyed working alongside. There was a steady warmth to Isabelle, a confidence that made everyone feel at ease, customers and coworkers alike.

Finished with the table, Layla approached the counter, neatly folding the cleaning cloth in her hands. Isabelle turned to her with a welcoming smile as she set two steaming cappuccinos down on a tray.

"Busy morning, huh?" Isabelle asked, wiping a strand of dark hair away from her forehead. "It always surprises me how everyone shows up at the same exact moment."

Layla chuckled softly, placing the cloth under the counter. "I know. It's like there's an alarm somewhere telling them exactly when to rush us."

Isabelle grinned, leaning against the counter. "Are you headed out soon? You must have a million things on your list with your business and the kids."

Layla nodded, a gentle sigh escaping her lips. "Yeah, a couple of stops at the market and then some planning to catch up on. I've got that beachside birthday party this weekend, and I still need to finalize the flower arrangements."

Isabelle's eyes brightened with genuine interest. "That sounds lovely. I don't know how you manage it all, Layla. Between working here, running your own business, and raising those two little bundles of energy, you're a superhero."

Layla felt warmth spread across her cheeks. "Trust me, I don't feel like one most days. I'm usually just grateful if I remember to brush my hair before I leave the house."

They shared a quiet laugh, the easy camaraderie a soothing balm to the usual frenzy of Layla's day.

"Well," Isabelle continued, "let me know if you need any help at the café or with the events. I'm always up for extra hours."

"Thanks, Isabelle," Layla said sincerely, touched by her coworker's offer. "I might actually take you up on that soon."

"Good. You should," Isabelle said firmly, nudging her gently. "Now get going before the market gets crowded."

Layla untied her apron and hung it neatly behind the counter, giving Isabelle a grateful nod. "See you tomorrow?"

"Bright and early," Isabelle replied cheerfully. "Enjoy your afternoon."

Stepping outside, Layla paused momentarily, the sun's warmth washing over her and gently easing the tension she hadn't realized she was carrying. She inhaled deeply, savoring the mingled scents of blooming flowers and the faint, tangy sea breeze drifting from the shore nearby. For just a moment, she allowed herself to close her eyes and absorb the quiet beauty of the island morning, a sense of peacefulness settling softly within her—one she had desperately missed in the chaos of recent years.

The island market was her sanctuary, and today it seemed even more vibrant than usual. Brightly colored awnings fluttered gently in the warm breeze, and vendors called cheerfully to regular customers passing by. Layla wandered leisurely through the stalls, each step bringing a renewed sense of calm and contentment. She first stopped at her favorite vegetable vendor, Mrs. Julia, whose face lit up as soon as she spotted Layla approaching.

"Ah, good morning, Layla!" Mrs. Julia exclaimed warmly, carefully arranging vibrant tomatoes and bundles of leafy greens. "You're just in time. Everything was harvested fresh this morning."

Layla smiled warmly, lifting a ripe tomato to admire its vibrant color. "Everything looks wonderful, as always."

Mrs. Julia chuckled softly, filling Layla's canvas bag with generous handfuls of crisp vegetables. "How are Mia and Noah?"

"They're doing well," Layla replied fondly. "Keeping me busy as always."

"Good," Mrs. Julia nodded, her eyes twinkling with gentle understanding. "Busy means healthy. And your event planning—still growing?"

Layla nodded, pride touching her voice. "Yes, slowly but steadily. I have another small event coming up. Beachside birthday this weekend."

"You always did have a knack for creating beautiful moments," Mrs. Julia said approvingly, handing the bag over the counter. "They're lucky to have you."

"Thank you," Layla said softly, feeling a warm glow from the older woman's genuine encouragement. She tucked the bag under her arm, feeling refreshed as she continued wandering through the bustling stalls.

Each interaction at the market grounded her, brief conversations with familiar faces offering snippets of genuine connection. She cherished these moments, finding solace in their simplicity and authenticity. It reminded her of what she'd come here to find—not grand adventures, but steady, quiet moments filled with warmth and kindness, reminding her gently that life, despite its complications, could still be filled with small, precious joys.

Reaching the fruit stand, Layla began carefully inspecting a crate of mangoes, her fingers gently pressing each one, feeling for the perfect balance of softness and firmness. Her thoughts were drifting lazily, focused on the sweetness she hoped to find inside the fruit, when suddenly she became aware of someone standing close by—a quiet yet noticeable presence.

Glancing up, Layla met the steady, gentle gaze of a stranger. He was tall, with an easy posture that suggested comfort in his surroundings, and his eyes—soft and warm—crinkled gently at the edges as he offered her a welcoming smile. Layla felt a sudden flutter in her chest, subtle but undeniable, and she glanced down quickly, momentarily flustered.

"I think these might be the best ones," the man said gently, reaching toward a particularly vibrant mango nestled among the others. His voice carried a faint accent she couldn't quite place, something melodic and intriguing. He extended his hand toward her, his gesture simple yet friendly.

Layla hesitated briefly, caught off-guard by the unexpected warmth of his voice and the sincerity of his expression. She looked up again, meeting his eyes, and saw genuine kindness there—no expectations, no pressure, just a moment of quiet connection.

"Thank you," she replied softly, finally reaching out to accept the mango. Their fingers brushed for a fleeting, charged second, and Layla quickly withdrew her hand, heat rising swiftly to her cheeks.

He noticed her slight embarrassment and smiled reassuringly, stepping back a little, giving her space while maintaining an air of openness. His gaze drifted toward her other bags, now bulging with fresh produce. He raised an eyebrow playfully.

"Looks like you've got quite a load there," he said, nodding toward her overflowing bags. "Would you like some help carrying those?"

"Oh, no, that's alright," Layla began instinctively, the response automatic. But she paused, considering his genuine offer and the quiet sincerity in his eyes.

Perhaps she didn't need to do everything on her own all the time. "Actually... yes, thank you. That'd be really kind."

He nodded, easily picking up two of her heavier bags, carrying them effortlessly as they stepped away from the fruit stand. Together, they moved slowly through the crowded marketplace, the bustle around them becoming a quiet backdrop to their conversation.

"I'm Ben," he introduced himself, shifting the bags comfortably, keeping pace easily beside her. "I'm here on a business retreat. Just a few days to unwind and reconnect, you know?"

Layla glanced at him with genuine interest, her earlier hesitation slowly fading into a comfortable ease. "Layla," she replied, offering him a shy, gentle smile. "I've lived here a little while now. I work part-time at the café we passed earlier, but my main focus is event planning. Small gatherings mostly—beach weddings, birthday parties, family celebrations. Nothing too extravagant."

"That sounds rewarding," Ben remarked thoughtfully, adjusting his grip slightly on the bags. "Helping people celebrate important moments. There's something very meaningful about that."

"It is," Layla agreed softly, surprised at how easy it was to open up to him. "But it's definitely been an adjustment. I moved here after... well, after some big life changes. Honestly, I wasn't sure if starting a business on my own was the right move, especially with two kids in tow. But it's turned out to be one of the best decisions I've made. It's been good for me. For my kids, too."

Ben looked toward her, his eyes full of gentle curiosity and quiet admiration. "You have kids?" he asked softly.

"Yes, two," Layla's voice warmed visibly as she spoke, her face lighting up with pride. "Mia and Noah. They've adapted better than I could have hoped. Honestly, this island... It's healing, for all of us."

Ben nodded thoughtfully, a quiet understanding crossing his features. "I've felt that too, even just being here a few days. It's hard to explain, but there's something about this place that just calms everything inside."

Layla smiled softly, meeting his gaze for a lingering moment. "Exactly. Are you finding what you need here?"

Ben chuckled softly, running a hand through his dark hair as he considered her question. "I think so. Life has been incredibly busy back home—I'm from New York. It often feels impossible to slow down. This island feels like the exact opposite. Everything here is slower, calmer. I run a small publishing house, and while it's fulfilling work, it leaves me with almost no chance to breathe. Here, even if just for a few days, I can finally just pause."

Layla laughed gently, feeling more at ease with each passing moment. "I can imagine. I've never been to New York, but from everything I've heard, it's all constant motion."

"It really is," Ben agreed with a sigh that carried both affection and mild exhaustion. "Exciting, vibrant, but always on the move. It's so different here. I envy you, living in a place like this."

They arrived at Layla's home—a modest, charming house just off the main street, its small front porch shaded by leafy palms and vibrant hibiscus bushes blooming brightly in the afternoon sun. Ben gently set the bags down beside the front door, stepping back politely.

Layla turned to face him, gratitude softening her features. "Thanks so much," she said sincerely, looking directly into his eyes. "I really appreciate your help today."

"It was my pleasure," Ben replied warmly, a quiet, sincere smile spreading slowly across his face. He paused, as if unsure how to proceed. "Maybe... I'll see you around the café or market again?"

"I'd like that," Layla found herself responding without hesitation, surprising even herself with her openness.

Ben nodded once more, seeming genuinely pleased by her answer. He hesitated only a brief second before speaking again, his voice gentle. "It was nice talking with you, Layla. Take care."

"You too, Ben," she replied softly.

Layla watched Ben walk slowly away, his figure blending gradually into the vibrant scene of the afternoon street. She lingered a moment, feeling the warmth of their unexpected encounter still settled gently inside her chest. Shaking herself lightly, she smiled and gathered her bags, stepping toward her home. As soon as she pushed open the front door, the familiar and comforting chaos of her daily life rushed forward to meet her.

"Mama!" Noah squealed happily, barreling toward her with unsteady toddler steps, arms stretched wide.

Layla laughed softly, setting the bags down to scoop him up, nuzzling her nose into his soft curls. "Hello, my little man. Did you miss me?"

Noah nodded vigorously, wrapping small arms around her neck. "Yes, Mama! Mia said you got mangoes!"

Mia appeared in the doorway, smiling brightly, her dark curls bouncing gently around her shoulders. "Well, did you?"

Layla nodded warmly, setting Noah down gently and handing Mia one of the canvas bags. "Yes, I did— perfectly ripe. Want to help me unpack?"

Mia eagerly accepted the bag, already peering inside. "Are we making something special tonight?"

Layla smiled, guiding the children into the kitchen. "Maybe some fresh fruit salad for dessert. Sound good?"

"Perfect!" Mia agreed happily, already pulling items from the bags, her voice filled with cheerful chatter as she carefully sorted vegetables onto the counter. "Did you have a good day at work, Mom?"

Layla hesitated, memories of the brief encounter at the market flickering in her thoughts. "Yes, actually.

It was a nice day," she replied softly, arranging groceries beside her daughter.

Noah, distracted by a ripe mango, lifted it carefully, eyes wide. "Is this one mine, Mama?"

Layla laughed lightly, gently taking the fruit from him to peel it. "This one is yours, sweetheart. You can help cut it up, okay?"

He nodded eagerly, his small face bright with delight as he watched her slice the fruit, little fingers patiently waiting to help arrange the pieces.

As they prepared dinner together, Layla found comfort in their small, easy conversations. Mia shared stories from school, recounting the details of her day with dramatic enthusiasm, while Noah interjected occasionally with his own cheerful observations. Layla felt a warmth expand within her as she listened to their voices blend together, creating a gentle, reassuring melody in their small kitchen.

Dinner passed peacefully, filled with laughter and simple joy, and afterward, Layla guided Mia through her homework, patiently helping her with math problems while Noah quietly played with his favorite trucks on the rug nearby.

When bedtime finally came, Layla tucked them into their beds, smoothing their blankets lovingly. Mia yawned softly, her eyelids heavy. "Mom?"

"Yes, sweetheart?" Layla replied, smoothing the hair back from her daughter's forehead.

Mia smiled softly, eyes already drifting shut. "Love you, Mom."

Layla leaned down, gently kissing her forehead. "I love you, too, sweetheart."

After checking on Noah, who was already peacefully asleep, Layla moved quietly back into the main living area. The house was calm now, lit softly by the glow of a small lamp. She sat at her desk, sorting through emails and event proposals, jotting down notes and marking appointments in her calendar.

Yet, despite the busy task before her, Layla found her mind drifting back involuntarily to the moment at the market—the gentle smile, the brief touch, the unexpected flutter of something she had thought was long gone. It was disorienting, but not unwelcome. It was, she realized, the first time in a long while that she'd felt truly seen.

Eventually, she stood and moved to the kitchen, pouring herself a glass of cool water. Leaning against the countertop, Layla allowed herself a small, tentative smile. She understood that it wasn't romance she was dwelling upon—not love exactly—but something simpler, softer, infinitely more delicate. It was the quiet realization that perhaps her heart wasn't entirely numb, that life still held small surprises and gentle awakenings.

Turning off the kitchen lights, Layla moved silently through the house, pausing briefly at the window to gaze out at the clear, starlit sky. She felt quiet contentment deep within her chest, a soft assurance that perhaps her heart, after everything it had endured, was slowly healing—carefully making room for possibilities she'd thought impossible.

She climbed into bed, pulling the covers up around her shoulders, settling into the familiar comfort of the night. As she drifted into sleep, her thoughts lingered gently on the stranger at the market—not because he meant something specific or immediate—but because he had reminded her of a part of herself she had nearly forgotten existed.

Tomorrow would be busy again, filled with café shifts and event-planning meetings, balancing motherhood with business, all the familiar responsibilities of her life. But for tonight, Layla allowed herself the luxury of quiet hope. Possibility. And the gentle reassurance that her heart, resilient and quietly brave, might one day fully open itself again.

Chapter 9:
Running From Home

Layla's hands trembled slightly as she arranged the final touches on the table settings. Her eyes flickered back and forth between the floral arrangements, the candles she had carefully placed, and the checklist in her hand. Today wasn't just any event—it was her first wedding on the island. The first time she had been hired to bring a couple's dream to life, to create something beautiful from scratch. She had done smaller parties and intimate gatherings before, but this was different. Weddings were supposed to be perfect, and in her mind, perfection was what would prove her worth.

The job had come to her as a bit of a surprise. She'd been working at the café for a few months, making small talk with tourists and locals. One evening, while serving coffee to a table of bridal party members, Layla had overheard them discussing wedding plans. Sofia, the bride-to-be, had been nervously sharing how difficult it had been to find someone who could handle the details of their small, intimate wedding. Without thinking, Layla had mentioned she had experience with event planning, and the words had tumbled out before she could stop them.

Sofia had looked at her with interest. "You do event planning?" she asked, eyes narrowing slightly in thought. "What kind of events?"

Layla, caught off guard but feeling an unexpected surge of confidence, had nodded. "Weddings, birthdays... I've been planning small events for a while. I'd love to help with yours, if you're looking for someone."

The rest was a blur—Layla left her business card with Sofia, and a week later, she had an email in her inbox asking for a proposal. It felt unreal. Was she really ready for this? But the opportunity was too big to pass up. Layla spent nights working through designs, budgets, and schedules, crafting the perfect vision for Sofia's day.

And now, standing in front of the tables that had once been mere ideas in her notebook, Layla felt both excitement and pressure building in her chest. Her future here depended on this wedding going off without a hitch. She had spent weeks planning every detail, from handpicking local suppliers to sourcing everything she could from island vendors—flowers, fabrics, cakes, even the music.

Her heart raced with the knowledge that this was a turning point. If she could pull this off, it could open doors—new clients, recognition, maybe even a permanent business. If it went wrong, though, she knew it could also shut everything down before it even started. Her palms were slick with sweat, but she forced herself to focus.

The venue was a small, seaside chapel with an open-air layout, where the wind tousled the palm trees and the scent of saltwater danced in the air. The soft hum of the ocean's waves crashing against the shore provided the soundtrack for this perfect day. The walls of the chapel were made of weathered stone, adorned with intricate, handmade lace, and the stained-glass windows caught the afternoon sun in bursts of vibrant color. Layla had been inspired by this venue from the moment she'd first seen it—this was the place where dreams were meant to come true.

But even with the beauty of the venue and her meticulous planning, Layla couldn't silence the nervous hum in her chest. She had worked with brides before, but this was a whole new level. Sofia, the bride, was anxious—Layla could tell from their conversations leading up to the day. Sofia was a local, and her family was well-known on the island. Layla knew this wedding wasn't just about two people coming together; it was a social event that carried weight in the community. Sofia's family had deep ties to the island, and Layla had heard whispers that this wedding would be discussed for months to come. That made her nerves even sharper.

Sofia had been friendly and warm, but there had always been an underlying tension in their conversations. Layla understood that. Weddings were intensely personal. They were full of dreams, hopes, and family expectations. There was little room for mistakes. The pressure felt heavy, and Layla had tried her best to reassure Sofia, but the bride's lingering doubts were obvious.

This morning, everything had started off well enough. Layla arrived early, double-checked the arrangements, and even helped the photographer get a few test shots. The weather was perfect—clear skies, and the kind of warmth that settled on your skin and made everything feel alive. Her heart fluttered in anticipation when Sofia and her bridesmaids arrived, looking radiant in soft cream-colored robes, their faces full of excitement and joy. Layla felt the nerves building but kept them at bay, thinking that once the ceremony started, everything would fall into place.

But there were cracks starting to form. She could feel it in the air. The flower delivery, which was supposed to arrive an hour before the ceremony, hadn't made it. Layla, trying to hold it together, quickly sent a message to the supplier, but her phone buzzed in her pocket without any response. She knew the timeline.

She couldn't afford a delay. Yet here she was—
waiting.

By the time the flowers were supposed to arrive, the
guests had already started trickling in, their laughter
and chatter filling the warm island air. Layla was
sweating through her blouse, her palms clammy
against the smooth surface of the clipboard in her
hands. She had started to arrange the table settings,
tweaking every detail with care—placing the napkins
just right, adjusting the silverware, and checking the
alignment of the chairs. Anything to distract herself
from the growing sense of panic that gnawed at her
stomach.

The delay in the flower delivery meant that there was
no time left for the grand floral arch she had so
carefully envisioned for the altar, the one she'd
pictured with soft white lilies intertwined with the
blush roses that would create an ethereal frame for
the couple's vows. No time for the delicate petals she
had planned to scatter on the ground, creating a trail
that led the bride down the aisle like something out

of a dream. Without the flowers, the entire ambiance was incomplete—bare.

Instead, she was left scrambling to make do with mismatched centerpieces—vibrant yellow daisies and dull carnations that she had no idea how to make work in her design. The delicate touch she had hoped for now felt like a distant fantasy. Nothing was coming together as she had imagined.

Layla stepped outside to look for the delivery truck. She could hear the sound of guests chatting as they found their seats, oblivious to the chaos brewing just behind the scenes. The warm sea breeze carried the salty scent of the ocean, but it couldn't clear the tightness in her chest. She scanned the road nervously, eyes darting to every car that passed, willing the delivery truck to show up, but there was nothing. Her breath quickened, and she checked the time again—fifteen minutes before the ceremony was supposed to start. The flowers were still not here. Panic set in as she pushed her hair back, trying to gather the scattered pieces of her calm.

Then, at last, she spotted the truck in the distance, rolling slowly down the narrow road. Layla's stomach clenched tighter with dread as it pulled up in front of the venue, an hour later than expected. The driver, a young man with a nervous twitch to his movements, climbed out of the truck. His face was pale, as though he'd been running on sheer adrenaline, but Layla didn't have time to sympathize.

"Sorry, Miss," he said breathlessly, unloading the boxes of flowers in a rush. "The shop had a lot of orders today. They just didn't have enough staff to get everything delivered on time. It won't happen again, I promise."

Layla's heart skipped a beat. The words "It won't happen again" echoed hollowly in her mind. She forced a tight-lipped smile, thanking him, even though the tension coiled tighter in her chest. There was no time left to dwell on the delivery. No time for questions. Only action.

She moved quickly to the boxes as they were unloaded from the truck. As she opened the first box, the smell of the flowers hit her—sickly sweet, but something else, too. Something wrong. The petals inside were wilted, limp, and the stems were already browning. Layla froze for a moment, her hands shaking as she pulled out the first bundle of flowers. These weren't the soft, romantic blush roses she had ordered. No, these were garish, bright yellow daisies, their petals already wilting. She pulled out another box, hoping for the white lilies she had carefully selected for their delicate scent and purity. Instead, she found a handful of limp carnations, their bright pink color clashing with everything she had planned.

Her chest tightened, and the air around her seemed to close in. The flowers she had imagined—carefully selected to match the romantic, elegant vision—were now completely wrong. Layla felt like she was drowning in the weight of the moment. She had poured everything into this. Every detail had been meticulously planned, every choice considered for its beauty and its ability to create a moment of magic. But now? She was holding flowers that felt like an insult to the vision she'd so carefully crafted. There was no way she could salvage the elegant look she had promised.

She wanted to scream, to throw the flowers away, and run. But the guests were beginning to gather, and the clock was ticking. She couldn't afford to panic now, not in front of everyone. Layla forced herself to swallow the rising tide of frustration. She could still make it work. She had to.

Layla quickly moved back inside, where the tables were still standing empty. She set the wilted daisies in the centerpieces, but they looked wrong—brash, out of place against the delicate china and soft linens she had chosen. She rushed to arrange the carnations, their heavy pink color clashing with the subtle pastels she had carefully selected. She could already feel the eyes of the guests—their confused glances as they walked in, the questions they would no doubt ask later about why the décor didn't match their expectations.

The wedding wasn't supposed to be about this—about scrambling to make up for mistakes she couldn't undo. It was supposed to be her moment. The day that would set the tone for her business, a statement of what she was capable of. A chance to show that she could handle the big events, the ones that mattered. But now? She felt like she was holding on to a thread that was unraveling.

Her breath quickened, her heart racing in her chest as she looked around the venue. The flowers weren't right. The colors didn't work. The vision was slipping through her fingers. And it wasn't just about the flowers—it was about everything. The wedding had been her chance to prove that she could make something beautiful, something memorable. But now, she could already see the disappointment in the bride's eyes. The disappointment that was bound to come. She tried to swallow the lump in her throat, but it only seemed to grow larger with each passing second.

Layla fought to keep her hands steady as she quickly rearranged the mismatched centerpieces. The guests were beginning to filter into the reception area, and she had to act fast. With every minute that passed, the pressure mounted. The bride would be expecting the grand entrance soon, and Layla needed to be ready.

She took a deep breath, trying to center herself, focusing only on what she could control. There was no time to cry, no time for self-pity. She could still save this. Somehow.

As she moved from table to table, adjusting the arrangements, she reminded herself that the little things mattered. The details—the flickering candlelight, the music that would fill the air, the laughter that would soon fill the room. Maybe the flowers weren't perfect, but everything else could still be beautiful. She could still make the day special.

When the final touches were made and the guests settled into their seats, Layla stepped back to survey the room. It wasn't what she had dreamed of. It wasn't the flawless event she had imagined in her mind, but it was still an event. And somehow, it had to be enough.

Layla had studied every detail about the island culture. She'd carefully curated the décor to be appropriate, respectful of the island's traditions. She had made sure the flowers were native to the region, the food was locally sourced, and the colors she had chosen for the tables reflected the island's earthy tones. But there was one thing she had missed—one key detail that would come to haunt her.

Sofia had asked for a specific blessing to be placed at the front of the altar. It was an ancient tradition, a prayer written in the local language, symbolizing unity, blessings, and the family's deep connection to the land. Layla had understood the significance, and she had promised Sofia that it would be included. But in the rush to complete everything, Layla hadn't taken the time to ensure the words were printed correctly, nor had she verified the layout that would honor the culture properly.

She had trusted her instincts. She had trusted that a simple printed sheet with the prayer would be enough. But this blessing wasn't just words on paper—it was a representation of the couple's heritage, their history, and their connection to the island itself. The islanders had lived and breathed this prayer for generations, and its absence was like a void in the ceremony.

As Sofia made her way down the aisle, a slight but noticeable furrow formed on her brow. She looked up at the altar, scanning the setup for the first time, and Layla saw the flicker of disappointment in her eyes as they landed on the missing blessing. Sofia's eyes flickered to the side, then back to the altar, and Layla knew immediately. It was too late. Sofia had noticed.

Layla's heart skipped. The bride's expression hardened, and her footsteps slowed just a fraction, enough to make Layla feel like time had stopped. Sofia's gaze shifted back to Layla, her face pale, eyes searching for an explanation, but the words never came. It was clear that Sofia was trying to remain composed, but Layla could see it—the confusion, the quiet hurt, the mounting realization that something was wrong.

"I thought the blessing was supposed to be here," Sofia murmured, her voice laced with confusion and disappointment. It was a quiet question, one that cut deep.

Layla's stomach dropped as the weight of the moment crashed over her. She had overlooked something so simple, something that was deeply important to the bride and her family. How could she have missed it? The blessing wasn't just a decoration; it was the heart of the ceremony, a vital piece of the day's meaning. She felt the heat rise to her cheeks as the silence stretched between them.

Layla opened her mouth to speak, to explain, to apologize, but the words wouldn't come. She wanted to say something that would make everything right, but there was nothing she could say. The moment had passed. She had missed the most important part, the part that mattered the most to Sofia. It wasn't just about the flowers or the centerpieces—it was the culture, the legacy, the family traditions that she had failed to honor properly. In that moment, she knew there was no undoing it.

She nodded, her face flushing with embarrassment. "I'm so sorry, Sofia. I'll make it right," she whispered, though she knew it was too late for that.

Sofia looked at her for a long moment, as though waiting for something more, but then she just nodded stiffly and turned her gaze back to the altar. Layla watched her walk away, the weight of her disappointment palpable. Sofia didn't say another word. She didn't have to. Her silence was a clearer indication than anything Layla could have read from her expression.

The ache of guilt spread across Layla's chest, suffocating her. She had promised Sofia that this day would be perfect. And now, everything was slipping through her fingers. She had failed. The ache of the moment, the sting of Sofia's unspoken judgment, was enough to make Layla feel like she was drowning.

After the ceremony, Layla stayed at the back of the venue, desperately trying to hold everything together. The guests were mingling, laughing, and taking photos, but Layla couldn't shake the feeling that everything was unraveling around her. The late flowers. The mismatched colors. The cultural misstep. Every mistake was like a ripple in the water, expanding and growing, until she couldn't even find a place to hide from the consequences.

Layla watched as the guests raised their glasses in celebration, their faces full of joy, unaware of how badly the day had gone behind the scenes. She wanted to smile, to feel proud of what she had accomplished. But all she could feel was the weight of her failures.

Sofia had been polite, but Layla could feel the tension between them, like a wall that had gone up. When she saw Sofia again, once the guests had settled into their seats for the reception, the look on her face told Layla everything. Her brow was furrowed, her lips set into a thin line, and there was something in her eyes that Layla couldn't quite place—disappointment, maybe? Or frustration? Whatever it was, Layla could feel it like a physical force, and it made her stomach churn.

"Layla," Sofia said, her voice trembling slightly, the calm façade barely concealing the emotion behind it. "I'm not sure what happened here. I trusted you to make our day special. But this..." She gestured vaguely at the reception, the flowers, the tables, the room in its entirety. "It's not what I imagined. The flowers, the colors, the blessing... none of it feels right."

The words hit Layla like a punch to the gut. Sofia's disappointment cut deeper than any criticism could have. She had wanted to be proud of this moment—to look at it and say, "I did this. I created something beautiful for them." Instead, all she could feel was the sting of failure.

Layla felt the familiar weight of self-doubt flooding her system. The room felt like it was spinning. Her legs began to wobble beneath her, and she reached for the nearest chair to steady herself. The last thing she wanted was to fall apart in front of the bride, but the reality was too overwhelming. She had let Sofia down. Worse, she had let herself down.

"I'm so sorry, Sofia," Layla said, her voice low and apologetic, the words tasting bitter on her tongue. "I did everything I could, but there were... delays, and I made mistakes. I'll make it right. I promise."

But Sofia didn't respond right away. She didn't shout, didn't cry. Instead, she simply nodded stiffly, a movement so subtle it felt like a dismissal. Sofia's face was hard to read, but Layla could see the tension in her posture, the way she turned away so quickly, as if she couldn't bear to look at Layla any longer.

Layla stood frozen in the same spot, the guilt washing over her like a cold tide. She had spent weeks preparing for this day, and now? Now it felt like a failure. She had missed the mark in every way that mattered. The flowers weren't right. The colors clashed. The cultural tradition had been ignored. She couldn't make any of it right now.

Once the event started winding down, Layla stepped into the back room, away from the festivities. She needed a moment to breathe. The weight of everything crashing down on her felt unbearable. The distant hum of the reception still bled through the walls, a constant reminder that the world was moving on without her. But for Layla, time seemed to have frozen.

The doubts, the whispers in her head, had already started—the same thoughts that had plagued her sleepless nights. She could hear them clearly now, louder than ever. "You're not good enough. You're not cut out for this life. You'll never make it." They echoed relentlessly, each word like a heavy stone added to the already suffocating weight pressing down on her chest. Every mistake she had made today seemed to pile up on top of her, crushing her spirit bit by bit.

She sank into the nearest chair, the soft fabric of her blouse sticking to her back with the sweat of the day. The room was dimly lit, with only the occasional flicker of light from the open doorway to remind her that she was still in the midst of the celebration. The guests were still laughing, still drinking, still celebrating a wedding that, for all its beauty, had never fully met her expectations. But here, in this quiet space, she was alone with her failure, and it felt like a thousand-pound weight on her shoulders.

A part of her wanted to pack up her things, walk out the door, and leave it all behind. She could get into a cab, head to the airport, and go home. Back to the life she knew, where things were predictable, safe, and where she hadn't set herself up for failure. Back to a routine that didn't require her to put everything on the line. Maybe then, she wouldn't have to face the reality of what had just happened.

But something inside her twisted at that thought, a gut feeling that she couldn't ignore. No matter how tempting it was to escape—to walk away from this moment of complete and utter failure—she couldn't bring herself to do it. She could hear her heart pounding in her chest, faster now, as the tears began to well in her eyes.

"I can't do this," she whispered to herself, her voice barely audible, like a confession to the empty room. "I can't."

It was as though a dam had broken inside her. All the frustration, all the anxiety, all the guilt of the day came flooding forward. The tears threatened to spill, but Layla held them back, not because she didn't want to cry, but because she didn't know who she was crying for. Was it for herself? For the failure that she couldn't seem to escape? Or for the dream she had so desperately tried to build, only to see it crumble at her feet?

The thought of packing up her bags and running back home was so tempting, so easy. She could tell herself it was just a mistake—an island wedding wasn't meant to be, the island life wasn't for her—and go back to her comfort zone. She could close her eyes, forget this ever happened, and try again somewhere else, somewhere safer. But deep down, Layla knew that if she did that, she would never forgive herself.

This was her chance—her one chance—to prove to herself, and to everyone around her, that she could do it. She had started this journey not just for the clients, but for her own sense of purpose, for the chance to build something that was truly hers. But now, she could feel that foundation cracking beneath her. She didn't know if she had it in her to keep going. But she had no choice. She had to keep going.

Layla was lost in her self-doubt when her phone buzzed. The sound was sharp in the otherwise still air, and for a moment, she just stared at the screen, unsure of whether she wanted to face the outside world again. But the message was from Isabelle.

"Hey, I saw you going into the back. Are you okay? I'll meet you there in five."

Layla hesitated, her fingers hovering over the screen. She had no energy to hide what she was feeling anymore, no patience left to pretend everything was fine. She couldn't bring herself to talk to anyone, but Isabelle was different. Isabelle had seen her at her lowest, and somehow, she never judged. Layla's thumb moved almost automatically as she typed a quick reply: "I messed up. Everything's falling apart."

She dropped the phone in her lap, staring at the cracked screen, not sure what to expect from

Isabelle's arrival. The room felt suddenly too small, too constricting, like everything inside her was pushing against the walls. She wanted to just be alone, to retreat further into her disappointment, but Isabelle was coming, and Layla knew she wouldn't be able to avoid it.

Within minutes, Isabelle appeared at the door, her figure framed by the dim light from the hallway. Her smile was easy, warm, but Layla could see the concern in her eyes. Isabelle didn't say anything at first—she just stood there, waiting for Layla to speak.

Layla took a deep breath, swallowing the lump in her throat. She didn't know where to start. The flood of emotions, the guilt, the shame, the helplessness—it was all too much.

"You're not alone in this, Layla," Isabelle said, her voice steady and calm, a grounding presence in the middle of Layla's emotional storm. Isabelle crossed the room slowly, her eyes never leaving Layla. "You've done a lot, and yeah, things didn't go perfectly. But that's part of it. It's a journey. You can't control everything, but you can control how you move forward from here."

Layla's chest tightened as Isabelle's words sank in. Isabelle wasn't judging her. She wasn't telling her it would all be fine, or that it didn't matter. Isabelle didn't sugarcoat it. She simply acknowledged that mistakes happened and that failure didn't define who Layla was. It was part of the process, part of the work.

Isabelle sat down next to her, close but not overwhelming, her presence warm and reassuring. "You've got the courage to keep going. That's the most important part," she continued. "The rest? It'll come with time. You're doing something really difficult. That's something to be proud of, not ashamed of."

Layla blinked rapidly, trying to hold back the tears. Isabelle's words were simple, but they held the weight of all the support Layla had needed in that moment. She had been so focused on what had gone wrong that she hadn't stopped to realize how far she had come. She hadn't just thrown herself into a new business; she had built it from scratch, piece by piece. Yes, there had been mistakes today, and yes, she had failed in some areas. But this wasn't the end. It was a moment—a painful one, yes—but a moment she could learn from.

Layla took a deep breath and nodded slowly, feeling something inside her shift, however slightly. Isabelle was right. It wasn't over. It wasn't perfect, and it might never be. But it didn't have to be. She could keep going, learn from this, and use it to fuel her next step forward.

For the first time since the wedding began, Layla felt a glimmer of hope. She wasn't giving up. She wasn't running away. She was going to keep going.

Layla stood up from the chair, wiping the last of the tears from her eyes, a mixture of exhaustion and determination creeping in. She needed to find some clarity. The mess from earlier still lingered in the back of her mind, but it was less about the chaos now.

It was more about what she could learn from this, what she could do next. The perfectionism that had kept her up at night had to be replaced by something else—resilience.

"I feel like I've let everyone down, Isabelle," Layla said, her voice thick with emotion. "The bride, the guests, myself..."

Isabelle shook her head, her expression firm but gentle. "The bride may be upset, but trust me, in a few years, she'll barely remember this. What she'll remember is the thought and effort you put in. The love you put into planning all of this. Weddings don't go perfect. But they're never about the flowers or the decorations. They're about love. The moment. And I can tell you gave her that."

Layla's chest tightened as she let Isabelle's words settle into her heart. She hadn't really thought about it that way. The bride, in time, would likely remember the joy, the commitment, and the celebration of love—not the details that had gone wrong. And maybe that was what really mattered.

Maybe the real success wasn't about executing a perfect day, but about creating a space where people could experience something meaningful.

She felt a flicker of hope, something small but real. Maybe Isabelle was right. Maybe she hadn't failed. Maybe this wasn't the end of her journey—it was just another step, another lesson. Layla wasn't perfect, but she was learning. And that was the most important part.

"Thank you," Layla said, her voice quiet but sincere. "I didn't know I needed to hear that. I was just so scared... scared that I wasn't cut out for this. For everything."

Isabelle smiled, her eyes kind and warm, offering a reassuring pat on Layla's back. "You're cut out for it. But you have to be kind to yourself. You can't grow if you're drowning in guilt and fear. That's how you burn out."

Layla took a deep breath and nodded slowly, her heart lightening just a little. She wasn't going to burn out. She wasn't going to let this moment define her.

She would move forward. It wasn't about being perfect—it was about learning, growing, and not giving up.

Isabelle's presence had been exactly what Layla needed. She could face the challenges ahead now. She wasn't alone. And that was enough to keep her going.

By the time the reception wound down and guests began to trickle out, Layla had composed herself, though the weight of everything that had happened still lingered. Her hands were no longer trembling, but a deep sense of exhaustion clung to her. The evening wasn't exactly what she had envisioned—there had been mistakes, things she could've done better. But the world hadn't ended. Sofia hadn't stormed off in anger. No one had booed her out of the room. Life had gone on.

Still, as she walked through the reception hall, Layla couldn't shake the feeling that something had been broken. Not irreparably, but enough to leave a crack in her confidence. The night had been beautiful in its own right, but it wasn't the perfection she had promised herself or the bride. The flowers hadn't been right. The blessing had been forgotten. And the air between her and Sofia, though polite, had a cold edge she couldn't ignore.

She walked up to Sofia later in the evening, after the last toast had been made and the final song had played. The guests were milling about, chatting and laughing in small clusters, but Sofia was standing at the center of a group of her closest friends. Layla caught her eye across the room, and Sofia gave her a small, strained smile. It wasn't the beaming gratitude she'd hoped for, but it was a sign that Sofia didn't harbor immediate, outward anger.

"Layla," Sofia said, her voice quiet, but with a faint edge that Layla hadn't expected. She sounded... tired. "Can we talk?"

Layla's stomach tightened. She braced herself, ready for whatever was coming. They stepped aside from the main party as Sofia led her toward a quieter corner. The guests were still busy with their own conversations, but the air between the two of them was thick with unsaid things.

"I know this wasn't easy for you," Sofia started, her voice tight, trying to keep her composure. "But this—today—it wasn't what I expected. I trusted you. I believed you could make our day beautiful. But now?" She paused, taking a breath. "It just... didn't feel right."

Layla's heart sank as she listened. Sofia wasn't yelling. She wasn't demanding answers. But the disappointment in her voice, the weight of it, was sharper than any direct confrontation could've been. Layla swallowed, her own voice faltering.

"I'm really sorry, Sofia. I know I messed up. I wanted this to be perfect for you." Layla's voice trailed off, the apology hanging in the air like an unspoken failure.

Sofia's eyes softened just a fraction, but the coolness in her demeanor didn't dissipate. She sighed, her arms crossing over her chest. "You know, I really wanted to believe you could pull this off. I know you put in a lot of work, but..." She shook her head, the hurt in her eyes palpable. "The flowers weren't what we talked about. The blessing wasn't there. And it felt like a lot of things were off."

Layla felt the sting of each word. Sofia wasn't angry—not yet—but the words were sharp. She wasn't ready to just forgive. She wasn't ready to smooth things over with a simple "it's okay." The bride had every right to feel this way, Layla knew. She had failed to meet expectations—failed to deliver on a promise she had made.

"I'm sorry," Layla repeated, her voice breaking. "I'll make it right next time. I swear I will."

Sofia looked at her for a long moment, the silence between them heavy. Layla felt exposed, standing there under Sofia's gaze. It was clear that Sofia was hurt, and Layla had no defense to offer—no way to undo the mistakes.

"I don't know if 'next time' means anything right now," Sofia said quietly, her eyes dropping to the floor for a brief second before meeting Layla's again.

There was no malice in her voice, but her words were a cold wake-up call. "I wanted today to be memorable for the right reasons. But I'm not sure I can say that it was."

Layla's chest constricted as Sofia's words cut through her like a knife. She had known it wasn't going to be perfect, but she hadn't expected it to feel like this. She hadn't expected the coldness that came from letting down someone who had trusted her.

Sofia took another deep breath. "Look, Layla. I'm not angry, but I'm disappointed. I know I can't fix today, but maybe we can talk later about how you can do better. I don't know... I need some time to process this."

Layla nodded, swallowing the lump in her throat. "I understand. I'm really sorry. I'll do better. I'll learn from this."

Sofia's expression softened, just a little, though the edge still remained. "I'm not sure when I'll be ready to hear about your next event, Layla. But... maybe someday. I'm sure you'll get there."

Layla stood there, still and silent, watching Sofia turn to join her friends. It wasn't the forgiveness she had hoped for, but it was a step forward—however small. The sting of Sofia's words would linger, but Layla knew that she had to accept this. Not every client was going to be easy to please. Not every day would go smoothly. But she had to take responsibility and move forward, no matter how difficult that felt.

As Sofia and her guests slowly departed, Layla turned to Isabelle, who had been quietly watching from the corner, the same comforting presence she had been all evening. Isabelle's eyes met Layla's, and she didn't need to ask how things went. The air between them spoke volumes.

Layla felt a weight lift off her shoulders, just slightly. The evening hadn't been flawless, but it hadn't been a disaster, either. There had been mistakes—yes, there had been plenty of them. But it hadn't ruined everything. She could salvage what had been learned and move forward. There was hope, after all.

"I guess that didn't go as planned," Layla said quietly, offering a small, self-deprecating smile.

Isabelle gave her a knowing look. "It's not the end of the world, Layla. Not every wedding goes perfectly. But it's a lesson. You'll get it right next time."

Layla nodded, grateful for Isabelle's unwavering support. Her mind still lingered on Sofia's words, but Isabelle was right. This was only one chapter in a much larger story. One mistake, one misstep, didn't define her entire journey. She had started this path to challenge herself, to grow—and growth came with failure.

"I can't promise I'll get it right next time," Layla said, her voice quiet but filled with determination. A faint smile tugged at her lips. "But I'll try. And I'll learn."

Isabelle nodded, her smile warm and steady. "You'll get there. One step at a time."

Layla took a deep breath, feeling the salty island air fill her lungs. The stars twinkled overhead as they walked away from the venue together. There was still so much more ahead, so much to learn. But for the first time in a while, she felt okay with the uncertainty. Tomorrow, she would pick herself up and continue.

This was just one chapter in her story. And for now, that was enough.

Chapter 10:
Hollow Girl Era

The rhythm of Layla's days had settled into a challenging but energizing pattern. Mornings were still early, filled with the hustle of preparing breakfast, getting Mia ready for school, and juggling her part-time café job. Yet now, there was a new pulse to her life — an undercurrent of possibility that carried her through even the toughest hours. It was the kind of quiet energy that only comes from having a purpose, and Layla felt it in the air she breathed, in the way she moved through her day, determined and steady.

Noah, still just shy of two, had become Layla's little shadow, his wide eyes constantly exploring the world around him. He had learned to walk, his chubby legs running after the dog or chasing the waves along the shore, but the world of school was still a distant thought for him. His mornings were spent in the care of a nearby daycare, a small, cozy place where he was surrounded by children his age, and Layla's heart swelled each time she dropped him off. It wasn't easy leaving him behind, but the daycare's warm atmosphere and the loving caregivers gave her peace of mind. She knew he was in good hands.

Her business was no longer just a fragile dream scribbled in a worn notebook; it was beginning to breathe and grow with each passing day. The rough sketches and ideas she had jotted down in quiet moments between feeding and bathing her children had begun to take shape in the real world. Layla had spent countless nights refining her offerings, reaching out to more local suppliers, and learning to navigate the complexities of running a service that demanded both precision and creativity. The transition from mere concept to operational reality was far from easy. There were hurdles she hadn't anticipated — supplier delays, last-minute cancellations, pricing miscalculations — but she met each challenge with grit and a willingness to learn.

Each new client was a vote of confidence, a step forward in carving out a space for herself on the island. The early clients had been tentative, their interest shaded by uncertainty about whether a newcomer like Layla could deliver. But with every successful event, every satisfied customer, her reputation began to solidify. Her social media accounts, once quiet and sparse, now buzzed with inquiries and glowing reviews. It was as if a window had cracked open, allowing fresh air and sunlight to pour in after a long, dark winter.

With the support of her small but growing community, Layla felt a quiet but steady surge of confidence. Vendors who had once eyed her with polite curiosity now greeted her with respect. The woman who ran the bakery downtown, once skeptical of Layla's fledgling enterprise, had recently introduced her to a new flour supplier who promised better rates and more reliable deliveries. Repeat clients offered referrals, and word of mouth slowly began to spread beyond the island's usual circles. Layla found herself invited to local business meetups and informal gatherings where ideas were exchanged and partnerships forged. She was no longer invisible. She was becoming known.

But it wasn't just the business that was growing — Layla herself was transforming.

The quiet moments with Mia and Noah took on new meaning. She listened more deeply to their stories, laughed more freely at their jokes, and found comfort in the little routines they created together. The hardships of the past — the sleepless nights, the heartbreak, the self-doubt — began to soften at the edges. Where once she had shouldered every worry alone, she now let herself lean on the small but steady support of friends like Isabelle, who always had an encouraging word or a practical tip to offer.

Layla's mornings still began in chaos — the scrambled eggs and mismatched socks, the forgotten homework, and last-minute lunch packing — but these moments were now punctuated by gratitude. The children's voices, sometimes loud and insistent, were also a reminder of the life she was building for them, a life full of hope and possibility. She was learning to let go of the weight she had carried for so long, the crushing self-judgment, and the haunting "what ifs." Instead, she held space for healing, small and imperfect as it was.

One afternoon, as Noah chased crabs along the shoreline and Mia collected seashells at her side, Layla felt a swelling pride that went beyond the success of her fledgling business. The sky was a soft blue, brushed with wisps of clouds, and the salty breeze tangled her hair as she watched her children laugh and play. Noah's legs moved with reckless enthusiasm as he darted after a particularly elusive crab, his small hands ready to scoop it up before it scuttled away again. Mia crouched nearby, carefully selecting the most perfect shells, her face scrunched in concentration. It was a simple scene, yet it held a kind of magic that filled Layla's heart to the brim.

It was pride in her own resilience, in the strength she hadn't realized she possessed. She was no longer defined by the mistakes she had made or the love she had lost. She was defined by what she was building

— what she was creating with her own hands and heart. The island, with its rugged beauty and tight-knit community, had become the backdrop to her rebirth. Each wave that lapped at the shore seemed to echo the rhythm of her own steady forward motion.

Still, the balancing act remained delicate. The café job paid the bills and kept the lights on, but it was the business that fueled her spirit. The pay was modest, the hours long, and the work sometimes exhausting, but the camaraderie among the staff and the familiarity of the place gave her a sense of belonging she had long missed. Many nights, she found herself poring over spreadsheets and contracts, her fingers aching but her mind alive with ideas. The exhaustion was real, but so was the exhilaration of taking control of her own destiny. She often sat late into the night, the soft glow of her laptop illuminating the cramped kitchen table where invoices and notes were scattered like pieces of a puzzle she was determined to solve.

In the quiet moments, Layla often thought back to the lessons learned from her past relationship. She no longer blamed herself or Jason for what had happened but recognized that growth came from understanding one's own worth and the courage to step into new roles. The heartache that had once threatened to consume her was now a faded scar, a reminder of how far she had come rather than a source of pain. This was not just about survival anymore — it was about thriving. She had discovered parts of herself she never knew existed: a fierce determination, an ability to inspire others, and a steady kindness that kept her grounded.

One evening, as the sun dipped low and the sky turned a deep shade of coral, Layla's phone buzzed with a message that made her heart skip. It was from a woman she had met through a local business association, a well-known event planner with connections to larger resorts on the island.

"I've been watching your work," the message read. "I have a client looking for someone who can handle a high-profile wedding next season. Would you be interested in discussing a partnership?"

Layla stared at the screen, disbelief mingling with cautious excitement. This was the opportunity she had been waiting for — the chance to elevate her business beyond the small gatherings and local parties. Her mind raced with possibilities and what-ifs. Could she really handle something so big? The thought was daunting, but the seed of hope took root. It was a sign that the hard work, the long hours, and the sacrifices were finally paying off.

As she shared the news with Isabelle that night, the words felt different. They carried the weight of possibility, of doors opening wider than she had dared to hope. Isabelle's eyes lit up with genuine happiness and pride. "You've earned this, Layla," she said. "You're ready."

The path ahead was still uncertain, the work far from over. But for the first time in a long while, Layla could see beyond the horizon. She could see herself standing firmly in her own power, a woman who had faced hardship and chosen to rise. The island, once a place of refuge, was now a stage on which she would step forward and claim her place.

This was no longer just her business.

This was her legacy.

Chapter 11:
Making Room

The warm glow of sunset melted across the sky, turning the clouds into streaks of fiery orange and soft lavender. Layla stood at the edge of the lush garden, clipboard in one hand, phone in the other, her heart thrumming with a mixture of adrenaline and quiet triumph. Tonight was the night—the culmination of months of tireless work, late nights, and sacrifices. This was the high-profile wedding she had been dreaming of, the event that would define her fledgling business and solidify her place in this island community.

The soft hum of classical music floated through the air as guests arrived, their elegant attire shimmering beneath the string lights that twined through the palm trees. The scent of tropical blooms and freshly cut greenery filled the garden, mingling with the salty sea breeze that whispered through the leaves. Tables were draped in creamy linens, topped with centerpieces of native flowers and flickering candles, casting dancing shadows on the faces of the guests.

Beside Layla, her new business partner, Elena, moved confidently, speaking softly but firmly to the catering staff. Elena's experience in event planning had been an invaluable gift to Layla, a lifeline as she navigated the complexities of large-scale events. Together, they were a force—Elena with her polished contacts and Layla with her infectious determination and local savvy.

Layla scanned the scene, her sharp eyes catching every detail. A waiter stumbled slightly near the buffet, nearly tipping a tray of carefully arranged appetizers. Without hesitation, Layla was there, steadying the tray with a reassuring smile.

"Thanks," the waiter whispered, cheeks flushed. Layla nodded, her voice low but steady. "We've got this."

The bride's mother approached, her eyes bright with tears of joy. "Layla, you've outdone yourself. This is more than I imagined."

The words sent a flush of pride through Layla's chest. She squeezed the woman's hand. "It's all for you—for them," she said, glancing toward the elegant couple exchanging vows beneath a floral arch.

The ceremony had been flawless—a blend of island traditions and modern elegance that left every guest captivated. Layla remembered the painstaking weeks leading up to it: negotiating with vendors, coordinating with Elena to align schedules, and countless phone calls to ensure every detail was perfect.

But even now, there were challenges. A sudden summer breeze stirred the candles on the tables, threatening to extinguish the flames. Layla moved swiftly, directing a team member to shield the candles with wind guards. Nearby, a guest mentioned that the seating chart had been misplaced. A quick check of her phone confirmed the chart was intact, but Layla knew a moment like this could unravel the whole event.

Her pulse quickened, but her voice remained calm as she reassured the guests and staff. "We'll have it sorted in minutes. Thank you for your patience."

Later, a server discreetly pulled her aside. A critical food delivery had been delayed—one of the main dishes wasn't ready. The clock was ticking; guests were already dining.

Layla exchanged a look with Elena, whose expression mirrored her concern. Without missing a beat, Layla pulled out her phone and called Marissa—the small-scale caterer who had saved her second event weeks ago.

"Marissa, I need your help," she said quickly, explaining the situation. Marissa promised she could whip up an alternative dish in record time.

Within the hour, a steaming platter of local seafood stew arrived, presented with flair. The guests marveled at the unexpected addition, many asking for seconds. Layla's heart soared—her quick thinking had turned a potential disaster into a culinary triumph.

As the evening wore on and laughter echoed through the garden, Layla felt herself relax into the moment. Her body was tired, every muscle aching from the non-stop pace, but her spirit was light. This was what she had worked for—the chance to create something beautiful, to bring joy, to build a business that was hers.

Between greeting guests and managing staff, Layla stole a moment to look out toward the ocean, the moon's silver light dancing on the gentle waves. She felt a profound sense of gratitude—a quiet acknowledgment of how far she had come.

Her thoughts flickered back to the nights spent hunched over her notebook, the early mornings balancing a part-time job and motherhood. The loneliness and doubt that had threatened to consume her now seemed like distant shadows.

Later, as the last guests departed and the garden emptied, Layla stood with Elena under the fading glow of the lights. They shared a look of exhausted triumph.

"You did this," Elena said softly. "You've built something real."

Layla nodded slowly, the weight of those words sinking in as she watched the candles flicker out one by one, leaving trails of smoke drifting gently into the night air. She realized something she never had time to say out loud: she had outgrown the version of herself who questioned everything. The doubts that had haunted her—the fears that whispered she wasn't enough—had slowly faded with each event, each obstacle overcome, each success celebrated.

That night, as Layla tucked Mia and Noah into bed, their soft breathing filling the quiet room, she allowed herself a rare moment of stillness. The journey hadn't been easy, and the road ahead was still long, but now she fully believed in her power— to create, to grow, to thrive. This feeling was no longer fleeting. It was steady, strong, and deeply rooted in her heart.

Chapter 12:

Let That Girl Burn

The morning light spilled softly through the slatted blinds of Layla's apartment, casting warm lines across her cluttered desk. A steaming cup of coffee sat forgotten beside her planner, its aroma mingling with the salty sea air drifting through the open window. Outside, the island was already stirring—vendors setting up stalls, children's laughter echoing from nearby playgrounds, and the faint hum of scooters weaving through narrow streets.

Layla sat quietly for a moment, taking it all in—the sounds, the colors, the rhythms of the life she had fought so hard to build. The weight of exhaustion from weeks of hard work settled in Layla's shoulders, but beneath it was a steady pulse of pride and purpose. The high-profile wedding they had successfully managed weeks ago had marked a turning point—not just for her business but for her partnership with Elena.

What had begun as a professional collaboration had blossomed into a stable, mutual relationship built on trust and respect. They had also become friends, sharing late-night brainstorming sessions and celebrating small victories together. Layla's business was no longer a fragile seedling but a thriving vine, climbing higher each day, deeply rooted in the community they both cared for.

She opened her laptop and scanned through emails from clients, partners, and local women seeking advice. The inbox had grown from a trickle to a steady stream—requests for event planning, catering, and now something new: mentorship. Women in the neighborhood, inspired by her story, had started reaching out, hungry for guidance on how to start their own ventures, how to step beyond the limitations they'd been handed.

One message stood out—a woman named Rosa, who had started a small handmade jewelry business but struggled with marketing and finding customers. Layla smiled as she crafted a thoughtful reply, sharing tips on social media, local fairs, and connecting with other entrepreneurs. It was a conversation that would soon lead to Rosa's first pop-up sale and a renewed confidence.

The transformation in Layla herself was undeniable. Just a few months ago, she had been barely keeping her head above water—juggling part-time work, motherhood, and the overwhelming anxiety of starting from scratch in a new place. Now, she moved with a quiet assurance, trusting her instincts honed by hard-earned experience.

That trust wasn't born overnight. It had been forged in the fire of late nights spent crunching numbers, negotiating contracts, and calming frazzled nerves during event disasters. It had been built in the silences between client meetings and the laughter shared with Isabelle and Elena over dinners celebrating small victories.

But the real growth had come from learning to take risks—not reckless leaps, but careful steps into the unknown. She'd turned down gigs that didn't feel right, said no to clients who didn't respect her work, and learned to ask for what she was worth without apology.

Today, she was preparing for a new challenge—a multi-day cultural festival that would bring together artisans, performers, and visitors from across the island and beyond. The event was a chance to showcase her skills on a grander scale but also to support the community she now called home. Layla saw it as an opportunity to give back, to create a space where local talent could shine and where women like Rosa could find a platform.

The phone rang, breaking her reverie. It was Elena, her partner and friend.

"Layla, the festival committee just confirmed the schedule. We have the prime spot near the beachfront. It's huge," Elena said, excitement threading through her voice.

Layla's smile widened. "This is it—the big one."

As the days unfolded, Layla threw herself into the preparations with relentless energy. Meetings with vendors, site visits, coordinating volunteers—it was exhausting, but each challenge was met with determination. She was no longer overwhelmed by the chaos but invigorated by the possibility.

One evening, as she sat on the porch with Mia and Noah playing nearby, Layla allowed herself a rare moment of reflection. The laughter of her children mingled with the distant music from a nearby street festival. The warm night air was heavy with the scent of frangipani and roasting coffee beans.

She thought back to the woman who had boarded the plane months ago—tired, uncertain, and weighed down by the ghosts of past mistakes. That woman had fought hard, stumbled often, and learned to stand taller with each fall.

Now, Layla was different. She had become a beacon—not just for herself but for others.

The mentorship circle she had quietly started was growing. Twice a week, Layla gathered with women from the community in a small rented space, sharing her journey, teaching business basics, and fostering a sisterhood of support and empowerment.

At the last meeting, Rosa stood before the group, her confidence radiant as she displayed her handcrafted jewelry. The room erupted in applause. Layla's heart swelled. This was why she kept going—the chance to lift others as she rose.

Amid the busyness, Layla noticed subtle shifts within herself. The self-doubt that once shadowed her thoughts had faded, replaced by a fierce belief in her worth and capabilities. She no longer measured her success solely by profits but by the lives she touched and the dreams she helped kindle.

One quiet afternoon, as she organized contracts for upcoming events, Layla received a message from Isabelle: "I heard the festival was a huge success. People are talking about your work. Keep shining, Layla."

She replied with a smile, fingers trembling slightly as she typed, "Thank you, Isabelle. Your support and encouragement always pushed me to find my own way. I realize now that everything happens for a reason. I'm grateful you were there, even when I couldn't see the path ahead."

That night, after putting Mia and Noah to bed, Layla sat by the window, the moon casting a soft glow over her face. The city lights were replaced by the gentle flicker of fireflies outside.

She whispered to herself, "I am enough. I am worthy."

The struggles of the past were no longer chains but stepping stones. Layla had learned that true strength came not from perfection but from persistence. From embracing every scar and setback as a lesson.

Her business was thriving, yes—but more importantly, so was she.

Chapter 13:

A Different Kind of Love Story

The sun was just beginning to set, casting a golden hue over the small apartment that Layla now called home. Mia and Noah were playing in the living room, their laughter a gentle soundtrack to the thoughts racing in her mind. Layla sat at the small kitchen table, notebook open in front of her, but her eyes were focused on the world outside. The rhythm of the island life had become a familiar lullaby to her—a contrast to the frantic pace of the city she had left behind. The distant sound of the waves crashing on the shore mixed with the occasional call of a bird overhead.

In the past, moments like this would have sent her spiraling into uncertainty—wondering if she had made the right choices, questioning whether her leap of faith was worth it. But not now. Now, Layla saw the beauty in this quiet life she had built. She had created something from nothing, carved out a space for herself and her children in a world that was still unfamiliar, and in the process, she had come to know herself in ways she never thought possible.

Her business was thriving. It hadn't been easy—nothing about this journey had been—but it was hers. She had started small, and now, she was handling larger events, working with bigger clients, and even collaborating with other women in the industry. Her reputation had grown, not just for her work ethic but for her ability to truly listen to her clients and offer them something genuine and thoughtful. She had a way of making even the simplest events feel significant. She knew it was because she poured everything into it—her heart, her time, her energy.

But what she saw in this moment, as she looked out at the sunset, was more than just the success of her business. She saw herself—how far she had come. The woman she was now, strong, independent, and confident, was far from the woman who had arrived here, uncertain and broken. The transformation had been slow, often painful, but it had been real.

Her thoughts drifted back to the early days when everything felt so fragile. When she first arrived on the island, her heart had been heavy with doubts. She had left everything behind. It had been easier to retreat into fear and uncertainty then, to question whether she had made a huge mistake. The future had seemed so unclear, and the past had been filled with too much hurt.

But she had pushed through. She had focused on the small victories, the tiny steps that slowly added up to something substantial. She'd built a foundation for her business, one that was grounded in authenticity, creativity, and a deep commitment to herself and her children. And in doing so, she had built herself back up.

Now, as she sat at that small table, she realized that the woman she had become was someone who had finally stepped into her own power. She had learned to trust herself, to take risks, and to see the potential in every setback. Her confidence wasn't just about what she had achieved—it was about what she had learned along the way. She had learned that it was okay to not have all the answers. She had learned that success wasn't about perfection; it was about progress. And, most importantly, she had learned to love herself—not in spite of her past, but because of it.

Layla leaned back in her chair, the warmth of the setting sun on her face. Her mind shifted to Mia and Noah. They were both growing up in a home that was filled with more than just stability—they were surrounded by love, encouragement, and a mother who was more present than she had ever been before. She watched them play, their energy infectious, and she knew that they would carry the lessons she had learned into their own lives. She was giving them something she hadn't had growing up—a solid foundation and the belief that they could build their own dreams, just as she had done.

Her phone buzzed on the table, pulling her from her thoughts. It was a text from Isabelle.

"How are you holding up?"

Layla smiled at the message. Isabelle had been there from the very beginning, offering encouragement and support, even when things seemed impossible. Their friendship had grown stronger over the months, and Layla had come to value Isabelle's perspective on everything—her advice on business, her honest thoughts on life, and her unwavering belief in Layla's potential.

Layla typed back quickly: *"I'm good. Really good. I can't believe how far I've come."*

Isabelle's reply came almost instantly. *"You've earned it. Don't ever doubt that. You've built something amazing, and you should be so proud."*

Layla set her phone down, feeling a deep sense of gratitude. Isabelle had always known what to say, even when she hadn't been sure herself. The bond between them felt like the strongest kind of friendship—the kind that was built on trust, mutual respect, and a shared understanding of what it took to get to this point.

But there was one more thing Isabelle had given her—something Layla hadn't realized until now: the belief that she could do it. That she could not only survive but thrive. That she could build a future that was entirely her own.

A soft laugh broke through her thoughts. Mia and Noah were now in a tug-of-war over one of Noah's toys. Layla stood up, crossing the room to intervene, her mind buzzing with all that had been accomplished. She was proud of them—proud of the family they had created here on this island.

As she crouched down to separate the two, Noah looked up at her with a bright smile, and Layla's heart swelled with warmth. She realized in that moment that everything she had worked for was worth it. The struggles, the doubts, the nights spent in uncertainty—it had all been worth it for this moment, for this life.

Her phone buzzed again, and this time, it was a reminder about a meeting with a new client tomorrow. Layla smiled to herself. Her business wasn't just growing; it was thriving. She wasn't just a businesswoman anymore—she was a leader, a role model, and an inspiration. She had become someone who believed in herself and the future she was building, and that was worth more than any business success.

She stood up, taking Noah in her arms, and looked out the window. The horizon stretched before her, endless and filled with promise. Layla's journey wasn't over, but it was only just beginning. She didn't know exactly what the future held, but for the first time, she wasn't afraid of its shape.

Conclusion:
The Wake

The sun was just beginning to set, casting a golden hue over the small office Layla had recently moved into. It was her first proper office, not the cramped corner of her living room or the kitchen table where she had once huddled with a notebook, fighting back uncertainty. This space, small but purposeful, was a symbol of everything she had worked for. She had secured a lease for the office just a few weeks ago, finding a small, brightly lit room in a low-rise building near the town's main market. The walls were lined with shelves filled with her files, client contracts, event planning books, and a collection of motivational quotes. A single window let in natural light, casting long shadows across the floor, while a sleek wooden desk stood at the center, now neatly arranged with her laptop and a few scattered papers.

As she sat at her desk, the quiet hum of the air conditioning filled the space, mixing with the soft clinking of her coffee cup as she stirred. Layla let out a deep breath, the reality of it still settling in. This wasn't just an office; it was her stepping into a life she had once only dreamed of. Her own business. Her own space. Her own identity as a successful entrepreneur. It wasn't perfect, but it was hers.

Her journey had been about so much more than just building a business. It had been about rebuilding herself. About understanding her worth, learning to embrace the uncertainty of life, and stepping into her power.

She looked at the photographs on her desk—images of her and Mia, Noah, and a few friends she had made along the way. Their smiles reminded her of what she was really building: not just a career but a future.

Layla thought of all the women she had met in the process, the ones who had shared their stories, struggles, and triumphs. As her business grew, so did her desire to give back, to share the knowledge she had gained and the lessons she had learned. She had come to understand that her story wasn't just her own. It was a story that could inspire others—other women, mothers, daughters—to take control of their own destinies.

In the quiet moments, Layla found herself thinking about the future. She didn't know if love would come again—and if it did, whether it would be with someone new, someone familiar, or maybe just herself. But for the first time, she wasn't afraid of its shape. She had learned that love, in its truest form, begins with self-love and acceptance. It wasn't about waiting for someone else to complete her—it was about recognizing that she was already whole.

As Layla took a sip of her coffee, the faintest smile tugged at the corners of her lips. She had built this life—this beautiful, messy, real life—and she was proud of it. The woman she had been, the woman who was broken and unsure, was no longer who she was.

She was more than her past. More than her mistakes. She was a mother, a businesswoman, a woman who had risen from the ashes of a painful past and was now, finally, standing tall.

The journey had only just begun.